CW00501983

**About the Author**
Dale Harrison is a self-published author. Previous works include two internationally selling books of poetry, both included in this collection, and his first novel, *Outatime*.

He currently lives in the market town of Stamford, Lincolnshire.

Copyright © Dale Harrison 2019

All rights reserved. No part of this publication may be reproduced, stored in a retrieval system, or transmitted, in any form or by any means, electronic, mechanical, photocopying, recording, or otherwise, without prior permission of the copyright owner.

All characters in this book are entirely fictitious and any resemblance to actual persons, living or dead, is purely coincidental.

ISBN: 9781095691700

www.daleharrison.co.uk

# The Life
# and
# Times
# of
# Could Be, Maybe
# and
# Other Stories

Dale Harrison

For Tessa.

May you forever shine.

*I'd rather be a could-be if I cannot be an are; because a could-be is a maybe who is reaching for a star. I'd rather be a has-been than a might-have-been, by far; for a might have-been has never been, but a has was once an are.*

**Milton Berle**

# Contents

### Dance

Bordering on madness,
Bordering insane,
An ever-changing life that always stays the same.
Freedom is the snake always devouring itself,
And as we burn in Heaven and send postcards from Hell,
Life imitates itself and the world collapses to the ground.
Accepting everything is something I won't accept,
I'll fight for everything you give me,
And I won't back down at those gates of hell.
Change is the nature of the world,
And as time teaches us,
I ignore every lecture.
Rebelling against every rule is what I will do if I must.
Who knows what becomes?
As we learn lessons from time,
Let us not worry.
Maybe we will be taught,
But will we remember?
If we can learn to love under an electric sky,
And tango in the sea,
We can dance,
And we can sing.
So, for you and me,
For the world around us.
For a revolution.
Let us dance.

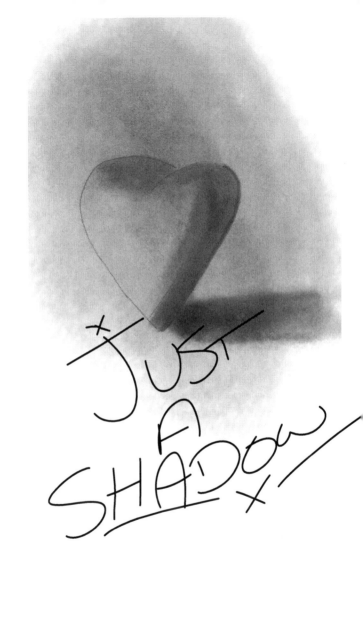

# Just A Shadow

## 1

$\mathbf{A}$s he lay alone in the cold bed, the damp and darkness surrounding him, Jude Goodman felt his breathing getting shallower. Wallpaper peeled off the walls around him, and the rough blanket that was pulled up around him scratched at his chin as it barely kept him warm.

What was left of his strength and energy slowly sapped away with each passing second, as Jude slowly sank further and further towards the hole of inevitability that approaches us all.

Jude wanted to keep his eyes open and see the world around him as it was coming to an end, but it was proving too tiring for him. There wasn't much to see in the darkness either, although there was a faint glow in the evening when the fluorescent light from the Soho street outside filtered through the grimy windows.

The room was empty, and there were no relics of remembrance for Jude and his life, his memories, everything that was his; it was all slipping away.

Jude didn't want to be alone when it happened, but he had no one left around him anymore. Well, no one that cared very much anyway. All his friends had dropped by the wayside, and with no family to speak of, Jude was alone. His neighbour, and closest thing to a friend, Joe, had popped in to see how he was doing, although that was more out of morbid curiosity than out of friendship.

It was a daily occurrence; Joe went to the shops, popped into Jude's bedsit on the way back, mainly to see if Jude was still in the land of the living and hadn't shuffled off this mortal coil, and read him the latest news, and then said his goodbyes after ensuring Jude had enough water and snacks at the side of his bed.

At 76, Jude couldn't argue that he hadn't had a good innings, and it hadn't exactly come to as a surprise that he was reaching the end of his life.

In his youth, Jude had tried to live his life to the fullest at every possible moment, riding the world like a merry-go-round, and he was never one to really regret things.

He had never given a thought to the lines that found themselves springing upon his face, and the hangovers that seemed to take longer and longer to recover from, until he realised as he grew older that he wasn't Peter Pan and after years of borrowing moments from the past, the time had come for him to pay them back, and with interest added on.

In between the constant partying, there were times that Jude had felt good and enjoyed life, without the constant company of alcohol of course, but those times were now resigned to the past as Jude had stoically accepted his fate.

Life would carry on without him, as it had a tendency to do, and he would be purely a shadow fading into the night.

Looking back on his days that had gone by so quickly, the old man, eyes of blue and hair of grey, sometimes wondered how his destiny may have turned out if he had just taken the time to think through things, instead of jumping in like a reckless idiot that had cost him so much happiness.

As he got older, Jude began to realise and understand the unintended irony of his name. He hadn't appreciated it when he was a bright-eyed young man, but as he had thrown away chance after chance, it slowly dawned on him who his parents had inadvertently named him after;

Saint Jude.

The Patron Saint of Lost Causes.

In Jude's life of mistakes and lost moments, there was one time that stood out to him more than any other. It was the most insignificant of moments to most people perhaps, but it was something that Jude always remembered.

It was his lost cause, and he had wondered about it since the day it happened. Somehow Jude knew. He always knew.

That was the day his life changed. The day his life revolved around.

He felt it, although he couldn't explain how or what he felt.

He had once heard that in death all of life's questions would be answered. Jude only had one question.

What if?

# 2

$\mathbf{T}$he sun was beating down on the warm streets of London as Jude Goodman walked through the heart of Theatreland and past Leicester Square tube station, striding along the bicycle lane to avoid the masses of tourists and musical lovers that crowded the pavements.

His brown hair was starting to show streaks of grey although his youthful looks remained, and he still looked young as the 39 years on this planet hadn't fully etched themselves into his skin. The stubble on his face, highlighted with patches of silver hair, glimmered as it reflected the light shining from the heavens above.

Jude wasn't sure why he was rushing through the crowds; he had no job to get to, and his relationship status wasn't something to write home about, even if he wanted to write home, that is. He had long since lost contact with his parents when he hadn't been interested in following his father's path as a lawyer.

The traditions that had been passed down had been ignored by the younger Jude in favour of a party and wannabe-rock star lifestyle. It was a life that he still liked to live, when he could afford it, although the people that Jude had grown up around had long since left the scene behind, and the noise he thought would never stop died a death when the punks grew up.

Hurrying to get away from the throngs of people that were scattered around the various theatres in the West End, Jude turned into Chinatown and forced his way through the even bigger crowds that dominated the streets. He would be glad to get away from all these people and have some nice peace and quiet to himself he thought.

Turning on to Wardour Street, Jude did a double take as he kept his head bowed towards the ground, ignoring the people around him. He always walked as if he had blinkers on, and this time he was glad.

Laying on the floor in front of him was a black leather wallet, thick and bulging with notes sticking out of it. Jude stopped in his tracks and looked around. The people around him were chatting on their phones, tweeting or constantly updating the world on their every feeling and movement, and all were too busy to pay attention to the black square that stood out on the pavement.

Without thinking, Jude stooped to pick it up, and immediately opened it up. There were wads of notes, although he wasn't thinking about counting it.

The first thing that went through Jude's mind wasn't to hand it in, or to see whose wallet it was.

In his mind Jude heard the beeps of slot machines, the clatter of a casino and the thought of extra money.

With no second thought the paper notes were swiped from the wallet, and Jude scurried off, checking around to see if anyone had seen his swift hands, although no one seemed to have noticed.

In his mind's eye he saw an image of his father. Jude sneered at him, glad that he wasn't doing what was demanded by a man who had never been there for him.

Making sure that the coast was clear, Jude hurried off to the newly opened casino nearby. Jude didn't believe in fate, but he took it as a sign that the casino was so close to where he had found the money. He had walked past it on many occasions, and he couldn't believe that he had been given this opportunity.

As soon as he had seen the money in the wallet, Jude had one thought in his mind, and he was going to see it through.

This single mindedness hadn't always boded him well, as his current lifestyle testified but one of the certainties of life is that time always changes, and the times always change.

Surely it had to be soon that his time changed.

Walking into the casino, it wasn't as busy as Jude had expected although that was probably down to the fact that it was just before lunchtime on a Tuesday afternoon. Not prime-time gambling time Jude thought to himself.

Walking through the casino, Jude didn't take much time in deciding where he wanted to go, or what he wanted to do; All on black, that was the only thing that occupied Jude's brain.

Heading straight for a roulette table, Jude took the wad of notes from his pocket and placed them on the multi-coloured betting surface of the nearest roulette table. The croupier changed the money for chips, and Jude was set. His pulse got quicker, and the adrenaline flowed through Jude's body. He could feel the luck pulsing through him, the knowing that his time had come.

It wasn't a case of *if* he won. It was *when* he won.

"No more bets please," came the call from the cashier as Jude could hardly wait to see how much he would win.

He hadn't counted the money he had found, but merely pocketed it before anyone could see, but he knew there were £50 notes, and now the chips were stacked high on the table.

Now Jude had a 50/50 chance to double his money, and he knew he was going to win.

The roulette wheel spun, and the ball clicked and clacked around for what seemed like an eternity as it tried to find its place in the world.

It finished making a noise and spun round on the wheel, Jude's expectation high in the air as his pulse quicken even further.

As the wheel began to slow Jude had visions of the ball nestled into a black bed, calling to him, teasing him with winnings and promises of a better life, of a future.

The visions passed as the wheel came to a stop and Jude had to do a double take as he looked at the result.

He couldn't believe it!

Red!

How could it be red?!?!

His brain was trying to tell him that there had been a mistake, but as the croupier announced the result and scooped the chips away, Jude couldn't help but look defeatedly at the would-be money

Thoughts rushed through his brain.

What had he done?? What if he had chosen red??

What if he hadn't gone in the casino?? What if??

What if...

# 3

Walking along Wardour Street, Jude Goodman was hurrying to get away from the throngs of people that were walking around Theatreland. As he walked in the sun, he did a double take as he kept his head bowed towards the ground.

Laying on the floor in front of him was a black leather wallet, thick and bulging with notes sticking out of it. Jude stopped in his tracks and looked around. The people around him were chatting on their phones, tweeting or constantly updating the world on their every feeling and movement, and all were too busy to pay attention to the black square that stood out on the pavement.

Without thinking, Jude stooped to pick it up, and immediately opened it up. There were wads of notes inside, although he wasn't thinking about counting it.

The first thing that went through Jude's mind was where the nearest police station was. It was time he finally started taking responsibility for his life, he thought, and doing what was right instead of pissing about, pretending to life a rock star life that he was never going to have. Better late than never, Jude supposed, it was time to grow up.

Jude quickly caught a glimpse of his father in his mind's eye and thought about how he finally wanted to do right by the man that hadn't always been there for him, but who was still his father.

Placing the wallet in the pocket of his thin, black jacket Jude took his leave and headed towards the first police station he could think of. Heading west towards Regent Street Jude fiddled with the wallet in the pocket, but he never thought or questioned if he was doing right. For one of the first times, he knew he was doing the right thing. He felt it.

As he entered the station, he had a spring in his step as he thought about doing the right thing. He spoke to the officer at the front desk who took Jude's details and filled out the paperwork, and then he was soon on his way, stepping out into the muggy London air, feeling good about himself and his good turn.

After a few days, Jude had thought nothing of the wallet after handing it in, and went about his business, or lack thereof, as normal.

On a slightly overcast Friday afternoon, three days after his good deed, Jude was walking past the Electric Ballroom in Camden Town. He had wanted to visit one of his old haunts and see if he saw any old faces that he recognized. It was a long shot, Jude knew that, but as he stepped onto the street from the tube station Jude' hopes had been dashed almost instantaneously and his spirits dropped when he saw the crowds that surrounded the area.

He knew, of course, that the area had become a tourist hotspot, and that the brightly coloured buildings and fiberglass shoes that stuck out of them were now so run of the mill that they were slowly becoming as much of a landmark as the Stable Markets further past the Lock.

Jude was doing his best to weave in and out of the crowds once again and to avoid getting caught up in the throngs of tourists when his mind flicked back to thoughts of his teenage years that he spent in the Market, close to the old rehearsal studios of the Clash.

He had looked up to the singer of that band, Joe Strummer, and always thought about a quote of his that he had seen spray painted everywhere; the future is unwritten.

Jude had always tried to live by that and make the most out of his life. It had never been a success though.

Suddenly he was pulled away from his youthful memories as his battered, old mobile phone started vibrating in his pocket.

He looked at the cracked screen and saw a number he didn't recognize. He hesitated, assuming it was someone trying to sell him something.

Ah, what the hell, he thought to himself and moved his finger to the green button.

"Hello?" he said as he weaved in and out of the crowds of people.

"Hello? Mr. Goodman?" came the voice on the end. "Mr. Goodman, I have a proposition for you…"

## 4

Jude walked nervously past the slot machines and roulette tables, the beeping and clicking just white noise to his ears. He wasn't sure what he was doing in the casino and was wondering if he was doing the right thing in being there. The phone call had been random and unexpected, although Jude guessed he had nothing to lose.

He headed towards the back of the casino, where a man in black stood next to a door with a keypad. The security guy watched Jude as he approached, then gave him a nod as he swiped a card through the keypad scanner and opened the door.

Ushered through the doorway, Jude walked down a narrow, wood-lined corridor, until he approached an open office door where he heard talking from beyond. He recognized the voice from the phone, and he listened briefly to the one-sided conversation although he heard nothing of interest. Stepping forward towards the open door, Jude looked through and saw where the voice was coming from.

Sitting behind a cluttered desk was a portly man, his dark, sharp looking suit in contrast to the white, wavy hair that sprouted from his head.

Oblivious to Jude looking though the doorway, the wild-haired man stood up and walked over to the window that scattered light into the room. He peered between the blinds, as if he was paranoid of someone watching him. Jude wondered even more what he was getting himself in for.

"Yeah, I don't care how you get it done! Just get it done!" came the shouting from the head looking out the window and back turned to Jude. He had his hand lifted to his ear, and it took a moment for Jude to realise that he had his finger on a wireless earpiece, something that Jude hadn't seen for a while.

As he finished talking, the man turned around and, seemingly knowing Jude was there all along, gestured to Jude to sit and he took a seat as well. Sitting opposite the man gave Jude the opportunity to examine the face of the gentleman who had phoned him as he was reminiscing around Camden Town, although there wasn't much that Jude could tell, as his Sherlockian powers of observation and deduction were pretty much non-existent.

The only thing that was obvious to Jude about the man in front of him was a scar that ran from his right temple to his eyebrow, giving him the impression of some kind of Bond villain. On the desk in front of him, amongst scattered paperwork, stood a golden nameplate, with John Newman imprinted on it.

Newman stared at Jude for a brief moment, as if he himself was using his powers of deduction to find out some unseen secrets about Jude, until he reached into the inside pocket of his jacket and pulled out an object that Jude recognized.

"This," Newman started, waving the wallet that Jude had handed in to the police, "is my son's. Now he doesn't care much for money, but this isn't about money is it? This is about honesty!"

He held his finger up to his earpiece again, looking at Jude.

"What do you do?"

Jude said nothing as he waited for the conversation in the earpiece to finish, and he sat looking at Newman. The awkward silence continued until the older man moved his finger away from his ear and gave Jude a nod.

"Oh, me? Sorry, I didn't realise!" said Jude, feeling a bit embarrassed. "Umm, I'm currently between jobs."

Jude was slightly ashamed to admit that he hadn't kept down a steady job for longer than he could remember and guessed that embellishing the truth wasn't really going to hurt anybody.

"Well, that's that sorted then! My assistant will be in touch," said Newman, and before Jude knew what to say, the casino owner jumped up, finger on ear and was shouting to his earpiece once more.

Jude started to wonder if his finger even needed to be there, or if it was just something the curious man did out of habit, or to make himself feel more exciting, as if he was part of some undercover organisation.

"Just get the guy to talk to me about that goddamn horse OK?!?!"

With those immortal words, Jude left the office with a job he wasn't expecting or indeed prepared for and headed out of the casino, into the smothering, midday London heat.

# 5

After working for three weeks in the casino, Jude was slowly adjusting to the life of a croupier. It wasn't his ideal job, but the thought of a regular paycheck felt good, and there were certainly worse ways to earn a bit of cash he thought to himself.

Jude had gone through a variety of jobs when he was younger, and none of them had ended very successfully. He had been unceremoniously fired from many of them after various mishaps, including a bout of aggression against a vending machine and, working in a bar, a verbal sparring match with a customer, which had ended with Jude drinking the customer's drink in front of them and politely telling them to 'get fucked'.

He had this time, however, a good feeling about the croupier job and was optimistic that there wouldn't be any such disasters.

As his stomach rumbled and spoke to him on the Wednesday afternoon, Jude was looking forward to his lunch break. Leaving the casino, he headed towards a coffee shop that was only a few doors down.

He passed the pair of tables outside that were occupied, as usual, by youths drinking some soya-milk based hot drink that Jude couldn't quite understand or pronounce, but which sounded suitably Italian. How many of these new, trendy coffee drinks with exotic sounding names actually came from Italy Jude wasn't sure, but he guessed that many people weren't so interested in authenticity anymore, as long as they had their caffeine hit with a hipster twist. Nevertheless, it was Jude's usual haunt when he was working and went through the doors,

It was busy, as it normally was on Jude's lunch break, but he was greeted merrily by the barista and took up his usual position on a stool that stood at the bar. A cappuccino was placed in front of him a couple of minutes later, and Jude enjoyed the caffeine and quietness that his lunch break allowed.

The stillness was broken by the sound of a police siren speeding past outside and Jude, as, it seems, every person anywhere has ever done when they hear a siren, stared to see what was going on. The car passed without event, but as Jude looked out of the window, in the reflection that stared back at him, he saw something, or rather someone, that made him turn his head.

Jude swung his stool around, and next to him he saw the most beautiful blue eyes and auburn hair that he had ever seen. Curly locks fell over her pale face and shoulders, and a small nose piercing glinted in the sunlight shining through the window. The young lady was writing, and Jude couldn't help but look across at her and what she was doing. There was just something about her that made Jude want to know more. He glanced down at the pen and paper in her hand and saw a list being formed.

"Hey, sorry to interrupt. How's it going? What's with the list?" Jude asked, trying his best not to seem nosy but at the same time wanting to seem interesting.

He wasn't very good at chat up lines , or even talking to women, and was hoping that she wouldn't tell him where to go, as had happened often in Jude's youth, although that was mainly down to what he said. He had found out the hard way that looking at a woman's cleavage and pronouncing loudly and confidently that 'I like you and your two friends' wasn't the best way to a woman's heart.

The girl looked round to Jude with a sad look on her face, her blue eyes tinged with red and make-up smudged slightly with the remnants of tears.

"I'm getting married in the morning," the girl said, a sweet Irish accent coming through her thin lips.

"Oh congratulations!" said Jude, trying to hide the disappointment in his voice. Always the bloody way he thought. "Wedding list?"

"Sort of," the soft voice replied. "I'm just making sure the reasons I should outweigh the reasons I shouldn't."

"Get married?" Jude replied, and was answered with a slight nod of the head. "Well the fact you're making a list tips the balance considerably. What's top?"

"My family are over in America and I'm not sure if I can leave them to stay here," came the reply, sadly.

Anna Moore had moved to England almost on a whim, when her boyfriend had been offered a job at a science laboratory.

Born in Dublin, her family moved to Chicago when she was a baby, and she had grown up in the Windy City. She had worked as a waitress at the Howl at The Moon Club in Chicago as she harboured dreams of being an illustrator. The music club wasn't the best paid job in the world, but it was entertaining, and she got on well with the guests there. The only night she didn't enjoy was the occasional open mic night when one of the regulars would unintentionally slaughter Beatles songs, but apart from that it wasn't too bad.

Her English boyfriend had got a job offer at a laboratory just outside London, after a few years working at the Sagan Institute of Science back in Chicago. Anna wasn't sure what it was that he did as it was top secret, but when he had wanted a change of scene, he had no trouble in finding another job.

She loved him, although they found it hard to make the most of their time together as he worked a lot. When she complained that he never made time, he told her he was working on it.

Anna never saw it though, and the years spent waiting on her partner had opened her eyes to many missed opportunities that she would never get back.

Sitting alone writing the list, Anna was having second thoughts about being away from her family and spending her life with a man who seemed married already, to his job.

As the stranger sat next to her and spoke, Anna felt relaxed for the first time in a long time, which was unusual for her. She wasn't one for depending on the kindness of strangers, but somehow it felt different this time. He had listened intently to her strange ideas for a children's book based on pumpkins, and laughed when she explained her fear of crumpets, although he was laughing too much to hear her defence that it was actually just the holes she didn't like, and she had laughed at his cringy attempts to make compliments.

As time passed, Jude looked at his watch and was grateful that he did. He had been lost in conversation with the girl sat next to him, and time had gone by so quickly as he listened to her stories of Chicago, although she could have said anything, and it would have sounded sweet in her Dublin accent.

He threw a five-pound note on the bar and got up to make his leave.

"I'm sorry, I've got to get going. Duty calls!"

"That's fine," Anna replied, slightly disappointed. "It was great to talk to you."

"Maybe I'll see you again," Jude said with a hopeful tone to his voice. "Good luck with everything."

Anna watched Jude leave through the door with a small grin on her face. She looked down at the list in her hand and screwed it up, and the smile on her face vanished.

## 6

$S$ummer had fallen on the streets of London, and Jude was still enjoying the benefits of regular income. His flat, inherited from an Uncle and with minimum costs, allowed Jude to live an easy, relatively care-free, life, without changing his lifestyle much.

On his varied two days off in a week, Jude enjoyed wasting his days with his three wise men, Jack, Jim, and Johnnie, and generally passing the time thinking about how life was being kind to him.

On a Thursday morning and feeling particularly decadent, Jude headed south of the dirty old river, crossing the Thames on Waterloo Bridge and turned towards the Southbank Centre.

Jude had been to the Roof Garden on a couple of occasions and enjoyed the view over to the London Eye; the sun shining down made him feel as if he didn't have a care in the world which, in a way, he didn't.

Sipping on his whiskey and enjoying the sun with his eyes closed, he felt the world around him go darker as a shadow passed across his eyes. Opening them, he squinted as his eyes adjusted to the bright light, and the shadowy figure that stood before him., and when his eyes finally came to, he saw a waitress with curly, auburn hair and blue eyes looking back at him, but he looked blankly, unable to place the face.

"Hey, it's me… the wedding list… from the coffee shop," said a sweet, Irish voice that Jude instantly recalled.

"Hey you, how's things? Fancy seeing you here!" Jude replied, hoping that she hadn't noticed that he hadn't recognised her to start with. "How's married life treating you?"

"Oh, we didn't get married in the end," came the sad reply. "I couldn't go through with it."

Jude felt bad that he recognised her more now she had sadness in her eyes.

"I'm sorry," said Jude sympathetically. "What are you still doing here?"

"Well he was the only way I would have been able to afford getting back home so I'm working here till I can afford my ticket home."

"Oh, there's no one who can help?" asked Jude, assuming her family would be queuing up to get her home.

"No, unfortunately not. I'll get there eventually though!" said Anna optimistically.

"Well I wish I could help," said Jude without thinking.

Why on earth would some random stranger want him to help he thought to himself. What a stupid thing to say!

"Oh no, of course not! I never thought…"
Anna didn't think she could finish the sentence
and wasn't sure she needed to.

The two of them looked at each other in
awkward silence until the waitress pointed at the
drinks menu that stood on the table.

"Can I get you anything?"

Jude picked up the menu and studied it. He
didn't know what he wanted, if anything, but he
was regretting his words and wondering if there
was any way out of his embarrassment.

After enjoying a couple of 16-year-old
scotches, Jude was enjoying his chilled afternoon
and couldn't help but watch Anna as she glided
along between the groups stretched out upon the
grass rooftop.

With the whiskey flowing through his veins
Jude was starting to feel more confident, and
without realising what he was doing, his hand
shot in the air and he called the Irish lass over.

Anna came over to him, and Jude wasn't sure
what to say; he hadn't meant to summon her and
was racking his brains for what to say; he didn't
want to embarrass himself again and suddenly the
Dutch Courage had given way to English
Stupidity.

"Did you need anything?" she asked him.

"Ummm, yes?" said Jude nervously.

What could he say, he thought?

Don't say anything stupid. Don't say anything stupid.

"What time do you finish?"

That wasn't too bad, said his inner voice. Could have been worse.

"At 8," replied Anna. "Why?"

## 7

Jude met Anna outside the Southbank Centre, and they walked and talked as they headed towards the London Eye. It was a slow, sobering walk for Jude, but he was appreciating listening to Anna's soft Irish tones.

She explained how, in the weeks since they had first spoke on the coffee shop, her fiancé had been cheating on her with one of his work colleagues, and how the wedding had fallen through once she had discovered the truth.

Big Ben chimed for 8:30 as the two of them reached Parliament Bridge and looked across the river, the Palace of Westminster dominating the view in front of them. The sun was slowly setting behind them and was casting an orange glow on the rippled water, which in turn illuminated Anna's face as she spoke.

"I don't miss him. He was a jerk."

Jude could see in her face that she wasn't convinced and raised his eyebrow.

"Well maybe I miss him a bit," Anna carried on, noticing the scepticism on Jude's face. "But you know, it's that old cliché. Let them go, and if they love you then they'll come back."

Jude took her hand as a tear ran her cheek, and with the other hand he wiped her face dry.

"And he never came back? Well, it's his loss," he said, trying to be comforting.

Anna tried to give him a smile and show him that his words of kindness were appreciated, although she wasn't sure if her smile was visible through the nervousness and sadness she felt.

When Anna had composed herself, they crossed the river and carried on talking. They headed up Parliament Street, past the gates of Downing Street, and under the watchful gaze of Lord Nelson. Their conversation soon took them to the corporate, neon glow of Piccadilly Circus and the groups of tourists that stood around as Anteros shot his eternal arrow.

Jude had heard when he was younger that the Shaftesbury Memorial Fountain, as the statue was also known, was not actually meant to be Eros, as he had believed his entire life, but in fact was Eros' brother, Anteros but as soon as he had learnt this new fact, Jude tried his best to forget it straight away. He hated the area and the bright glow of consumerism that dominated the square. It was only that he had been so caught up in talking to Anna that he hadn't even realised where they had been walking. It was only when Jude saw the fountain ahead of him that he remembered the useless information that for some reason had stuck with him.

The two of them stopped and stood under the small statue as it gazed down upon them, and though the crowds shuffled by them, the hustle and bustle seemed to be blocked out as they looked into each other's eyes. Jude had an idea what was coming, although with the location they stood at he felt like he was a character in a film or a book, with the little cherub's arrow pointing straight at him and the Irish girl who was new to him, but who he felt he had gotten to know so well.

Anna wasn't the tallest of girls and she found herself standing on her tiptoes opposite Jude as she reached up to grab his cheeks and pulled them towards her. They kissed as the lights of the adverts exploded over their heads, and Jude felt like he was on drugs as happiness overwhelmed him.

Later that night Jude walked Anna back to the small apartment she was staying at in Kensington and took a slow walk back to his small flat. It was after midnight when he found himself walking through the streets of Soho on his way home, and there was something in the quiet streets that Jude found comforting.

After the hustle and bustle of the crowds the new lovers had been surrounded with earlier, the peacefulness enabled Jude to gather his thoughts. He had a thousand feelings rushing through his head, all of them good, and, not for the first time in the last few months, life seemed to treating

Jude well and things seemed to be going right. It was a feeling he was slowly getting used to, and long may it last he thought to himself as the neon glow reflected off his tired eyes.

**8**

$A$fter a few days at work, and back and forth texting between himself and Anna Moore, Jude found himself walking along Waterloo Bridge, an envelope in his hand, as the sun was setting, basking in an orange glow that had been made famous in a song so many years ago. Heading down the steps, he sat on a bench outside the Southbank Centre, waiting for his new-found love to finish work at the rooftop terrace bar where fate had worked its magic and brought the two of them together for a second time.

As Anna finished walked and headed out the door, she wasn't expecting to see Jude there, and the happiness that appeared on her face was apparent to Jude and he was overjoyed to see her. She held him and tight and planted a kiss on his lips, her left leg raised in the air as women tend to do.

Why do they do that Jude thought? Strange.

As she let him go, Jude brought up the envelope in his hand and awkwardly and nervously gave it to her. A puzzled look came over her face and she examined it.

"What's this?"

"Just a little something for you," replied Jude, a nervous look on his face.

Anna ripped open the envelope and took out what looked like a ticket of some kind. She inspected it further and realised it was a plane ticket.

One way. To O' Hare International, Chicago.

Her face dropped, and a puzzled and upset expression set itself up on Anna's face.

"W,w,what's this?? Are, are you trying to get rid of me??" she stammered, unsure what to think.

"No, no, of course not!" replied Jude.

"Well I don't know what to say," said Anna, completely lost for words.

"Well you could say thanks," came Jude's answer.

"Thanks…" she replied.

"Or you could say that you don't need it anymore. That you have found a reason to stay," Jude said, trying the hide the sense of dread that had come over him as he tried to ignore the tears that were welling in Anna's eyes.

"I could… But I can't. This is so sweet of you, but I really need to get back home."

The eyeliner around Anna's eyes began to smudge as tears began to roll down her face.

"Here, take it. I, I don't deserve this," Anna said as she held the ticket back towards Jude and tried to push it into his hands.

Jude took her hands in his, clasped them around the plane tickets, gave Anna a peck of the cheek and turned to walk away.

The tears started to run down Jude's cheeks as he walked away, while Anna stood and watched him go. He daren't turn around and look at her. It would hurt him too much to see Anna's pretty face, knowing that he had to give it up and leave her behind.

Jude took a long walk around the streets of Soho that night, trying to clear some of confusing thoughts that scattered themselves across his brain; Why did he give her the ticket? How did he think, out of everything, that that would be the best way to show her he cared? What was wrong with flowers, or chocolates, or anything else that 'normal' people give?

Jude was cursing himself for being stupid, and as soon as he got back to his flat, he poured a himself a whiskey as he wished to turn back time.

One drink slowly became a few as a whirlpool began to spin in Jude's head, regret dominated his mind and thoughts of Anna were replaced with self-pity and loneliness, and Jude asking himself, what if…

## 9

Jude had gone back to work after drowning his sorrows on the two days he had off. He hadn't spoken to Anna and had resisted the urge to contact her. She had phoned him a few times although Jude had ignored the phone. It was still hurting him, and he was still annoyed with himself for even thinking that it had been a good idea.

Although their relationship had been very short lived, Jude had begun to get a good feeling about the two of them. They seemed to have so much in common, and time passed like lightning when they were together but, alas, it was obviously not meant to be, he felt.

Jude was standing by the roulette wheel in a world of his own, running on autopilot. It was once again a quiet afternoon, and Jude was struggling to keep his mind on the job and away from Anna, although there wasn't so much for him to do anyway.

Standing behind the table, Jude had his hand on the wheel, and asked if there were any more bets. As he did so, a hand laid down what looked to be a piece of paper on the roulette table. The manicured nails shone a light blue and stood out against the black and red squares on the green canvas. Jude stared at the paper and realised what it was; it was the same paper that he had given away only a few days earlier.

Looking up from the table, Jude saw the whitest grin staring back at him from a pale face, and instantly he started smiling himself.

"I think I've found my reason to stay," said the sweetest Irish accent, a voice that was music to Jude's ears.

The next few months and years went by in a blur for Jude Goodman and Anna Moore. When she had decided to stay in England, Anna had immediately gone to Jude to tell him and hadn't regretted it one bit. The connection they had proved to be everlasting, and within six months she had moved into Jude's flat in Soho. She had got a job as an illustrator for children's books, putting to use a talent that she had as a teenager but which she had never been encouraged to use in her previous relationship.

It was on the one year anniversary of Jude taking that fateful trip to the café where Anna was making the list of reasons for her wedding that he had proposed, underneath the statue of Anteros, of all places. Jude had finally found a positive in that consumer central of Piccadilly Circus that he had always hated.

The wedding that occurred a few months later was followed by a honeymoon in Hawaii and a two-week vacation in Chicago as Jude got to know the in-laws better. He had met them at the wedding of course, but there was so much going on, and Jude was trying to catch up with his mother and father, who had been invited as a surprise by Anna.

Jude was grateful that she had invited them; he was too stubborn to swallow his pride and do it himself, even though he had wanted to. To him that was just another reason why Anna was perfect for him. She understood him even when he didn't speak, and they had a bond that Jude had never felt or understood before.

After the wedding, it was only a matter of time until Anna became pregnant, and they became the proud parents of a baby boy. Parenthood had never been high on Jude's priorities, but with Anna everything just seemed… well just seemed right.

That was thing, Jude often thought. It just seems right.

## 10

$A$s he lay alone in the warm bed, the sun shone dimly through the curtains, and to Jude Anna looked like she had a halo as she was holding his hand, illuminated by the outside light. He was squinting and struggling to see but he wanted to view her as much as he could. Jude's eyesight was failing him in his later years, but although he couldn't see Anna as well as he used to be able to, his memories were crystal clear.

She was an angel to him, and the years they had spent together since that fateful lunch break so many years ago had brought so much happiness to Jude.

The memories and remembrances of their life together adorned the walls, with photos of their wedding day, their only child Nicholas, his graduation and wedding. Pictures of Jude and Anna's grandchildren were everywhere as they smiled at their grandparents through pictures from another time.

Jude felt his breathing getting shallower with each passing breath. He wanted to keep his eyes open and see the world around him as it was coming to an end, but it was proving too tiring for him. What was left of his strength and energy slowly sapped away with each passing second, as

Jude slowly sank further and further towards the hole of inevitability that approaches us all.

He had tried to prepare himself for the end, and tried not to be scared, but it wasn't working. The thought of Anna being on her own scared Jude, and he didn't want to leave her.

That was the main thing he feared, he thought. He could remember life before Anna, before their life had snowballed into a life of happiness, smiles and joy. To Jude he had already died once before, albeit symbolically, on the day they had met, as he started a new life, and Anna had been the reason for that.

Jude managed to open his eyes once more and looked at Anna as she gave him a little smile, stroked his face and kissed his hand. Her eyes were still as blue as Jude remembered when they first met, and although the red hair had long since lost its colour, to Jude, Anna Goodman was still perfect.

"Thank you," he managed to say in a dry raspy voice as he looked up at the woman who had changed his life, and with those two words, Jude closed his eyes again.

The end had come, and Jude was ready for it.

As he opened his eyes to look at his angel once more, for the final time, the room was dark, and Jude's shallow breathing caused tiny puffs of steam to come from his mouth and rise from the rough blanket that covered him. He was alone, the walls around him were blank, and a dull glow came in from the Soho street outside. Jude wondered for a split second what was happening, and he realised as he drew his last breath and closed his eyes for the final time to become a shadow fading in the night, a knowing smile on his face; a grim smile of realisation.

There is no point in looking back, you don't get a second chance, and life is full of what ifs.

# *Tomorrow, Today*

# Hey You...

Everything that you thought you know,
Ripped apart in an instance.
Everything was planned out, but now is
Upside down.
Moving forward is difficult when the world is stuck
in reverse.
The people who become who they once were,
Wasting the years of their lives.
Maybe it would be better to stand still, than become
That shadow of one's self.
Blank stares replacing the spark in the eye,
A shell-shocked casualty of circumstance.
At least the strong can support each other,
While the weak prop each other up, like pillars of
straw.
Simple thoughts of short-term acts,
Ignoring the world around.
No dream catcher will take away the nightmares to
come,
In a world hexed with regret.
Isn't it strange to think,
When the person is offered the keys to world,
They would prefer to throw that key away,
And trap themselves in a box forever?
It makes me laugh to think,
That forever now that person will always be just
lines in a book,
And photographs in the trash.
A black hole in the memories of the past,

And nothing to the future.
A footnote in history and
An insignificant blot on the annals of time.

# An Open Letter to The Past I

I'll be honest,
I felt fucked.
I had given so much of my life,
And to have it thrown away like that,
It hurt.
But after seeing and realizing how things are,
How I have moved on,
The progress I have made as a person,
I am, in a strange way, grateful.
I don't have to run after undeserved tears,
And selfish thoughts aren't my fault.
I am happy I knew sooner rather than later,
Before I had confessed my love to the world.
I will never be ashamed of feelings, but I am glad.
Glad that I didn't waste money, or time, or too
much effort
On you, such an insignificant thing.
I will certainly never forget a single day
But I will only say that,
Now I am happy.
Life is good, and long may it continue.
For that maybe I should be thankful.
And I will be.
But not to you.
You are a nothingness to me,
A blight upon my life
And a stain upon my soul.
No one needs cheap words and lies,
Certainly not me.

So, to finish off,

Thank you.

And fuck off.

## A Sad Truth

I confess my loneliness,
To you my only friend,
Standing with me, side by side,
Until the bitter end.

When the darkest hour comes near,
And nightmares are here to stay,
You catch those thoughts and hold them close,
And take those dreams away.

We have been through everything,
Two brothers in arms,
And again, I ask for your help,
Keep me safe from harm.

The only one I can depend on,
The only one I trust,
I'll run to the end of the world for you,
Do anything that I must.

I know you are always there,
From happiness to tears,
Here's to you, my oldest friend;
My love letter to beers.

## Women According to Sir David

Caught in a web, a helpless fly struggles
unsuccessfully while the predator approaches.
The female may look small,
But be warned.
She is very dangerous.
She will devour your life, and leave you with
nothing, until there is nothing left,
And then she walks away, leaving you for dead.

Hidden in the background,
Disguised and camouflaged,
The snake lies in wait until...
She attacks her prey.
Holding.
Smothering.
Not letting go.
Only when she has had enough are you released.
A snake with tits.

## Survival

A perfect sphere,
Balanced on the finest point.
The most destructive things cannot knock it over,
But the smallest thing can break it,
Unbalance the sphere for Eternity.
We need to keep our balance,
For everyone's sake.

## Millionaire

If I had a tiger for every time I did some stupid,
I could open a zoo.

If I had a fish for every time I said something I
regret,
I could open an aquarium.

If I had a pound for every time I was wrong,
I'd be a self-made millionaire.

If I had a sloth for every time I was sad,
I would be happy.

## Alone

From the golden moment I met you,
You left your footprints in my heart.
The imprints of your beauty;
The thing that tears me apart.
I had never found such comfort,
Never knew it existed,
And now it has been taken away,
I just feel broken and twisted.

# Cauldron Nights…

A glorious sunset hit me that evening.
A wonderful baptism on a day of reckoning,
The dawning of something new…

I have drunk until daybreak with barflies and
vagabonds,
Made company with strangers,
Danced with whores,
And seen junkies on their concrete beds.
I have been in the gutter, but not looking at stars,
Just my broken teeth being washed away.
So many stories to tell, and if walls could talk,
What would they say about me?
Sat with Traubert in a dark, smoke-filled bar,
Whiskey glasses stacked up in front of me,
Reaching up to make friends with the cigarette
stained ceiling.
In our Church the holy water never stopped
flowing, for us,
The disciples of inebriation.
Stained glass windows of whiskey and blood,
Worshipping the patron saint of the lost,
As we steeped our lungs with beer.
The blonde that cried at the bar turned into a
tobacco brunette,
Flirting with receding Hairlines for one last shot of
happiness.
Gordon and his tonic stemmed the flow of
loneliness,

If only for an hour.
An interlude in the nightly theatre show.
The scribbled graffiti telling us stories
Of the early hour affairs,
Of being drunk on love and wine,
Until the sun washed the feelings away.
Was I stumbling when I walked, or was the floor
uneven?
Or had my shoes had been drinking?
That must be it.
Getting lost in a box,
Distracted by the neon glow,
Lighting up the cracks on the skin that take you by
surprise.
Who frowned me this face?
Lines just appeared,
And the only eternal youth
Is the 16-year-old Scotch that keeps you company
On a grey Sunday morning.
How did Saturday turn into this?
I'm sweeping the ghosts away,
But the spirits still remain.
Early morning suitcase packing to run away,
Mind racing with blank thoughts.
Now come on Mr D, don't laugh at me like that,
Or you will find that I'll empty you out,
Then who will be crying?
I planted a garden that never grew,
Cut myself on thorns,
Lost weeks and months,
Stacking up like empty barrels.

A broken head,
The remnants of an eternal hangover.
Living every day like a holiday,
Not worrying about a thing.
Call up the judge to find I'm guilty,
But innocent of every charge.

## ...And Bright New Days.

Then that light shone down on me,
That said it is time for something new.
No revelations, no epiphany,
Just a yearning for change.
Getting better every day and healing ourselves.
New beginnings and new chapters,
Because nothing ever ends.
Stories never end;
They are eternal, being acted out and repeated,
Every day, the world over.
Stories don't end.
Chapters begin anew,
But the story lasts forever,
In memories, in photographs,
In snapshots of time,
Capturing that moment when everything was ok.
But isn't everything always ok?
When all is said and done, it must be.
From nothing can come a spark,
Lighting the fuse of change,
Igniting our hopes and dreams,
And forging our brand-new future.
Standing strong, and walking tall,
We can leave every problem we have behind,
As we search for a brave new world.
We write a new chapter,
Draw a line under the past,
Never forgetting the people we once were,
But changing to begin a life anew.

Time costs us nothing,
So why should we save it?
Live every day like a holiday,
Even when the sun doesn't shine.
There is only an inch of daylight left.
No need for worries as long as you live it right.
We never have to hide away from the world,
When it is our world to shape and do as we will.
No one can tell us how to write our chapters,
Or our stories: It is our decision.
My garden grows more with every second that I live.
I frowned me this face,
Worrying about insignificance and nothingness,
Until I saw that as long as feet are moving
And my heart is beating,
The sun will always shine on me,
And every day is the first day of my life.

# Open Your Eyes

Swallow a bird,
If it makes you sing.
Kill an angel,
If it makes you pure.
Embrace a shadow,
If it makes you believe
Write a line,
If it makes you learn.
Reveal your secrets,
If it makes you free.
Change a river's course,
If it makes you feel special.
Create a new Christmas,
If it brings you spirit.
But don't close your eyes,
Because you won't see a thing.

**The World and Yourself**

Lost amidst a sea of grace,
Look at your reflection.
Does it have a face?
Disappear into a world of your own,
Where thoughts and words are to be left alone.
Sometimes you can feel unloved and empty,
But take a look at that face and see plenty.
The one that you love, and madly adore,
Is standing beside you and loving you more.

# An Sibin

*Dancing and drinking just to pass the time,*
*In a couple of hours, I'm on whiskey and wine.*
*Won't be long until the time that I'm fucking high,*
*And when it gets to fucked o'clock,*
*You know I'm doing right.*

Serpent eyes are on the stage,
Heart is frozen in a fit of rage,
Scared as hell,
You can't tell,
I don't act my fucking age.

Well Chelsea's with her dagger,
And I don't want to go there,
Scared as shit,
About that hit,
I shouldn't even care.

You can save my soul,
As long as I play the fool,
Thinking of you,
Is never true,
Living by one fucking rule.

Lola's dancing at the bar,
George is drinking from a jar,
Life in a fast lane,
Giving everyone pain,
Destroy the world from afar.

Fuck Lucy and her rock and roll,
Living like outlaws is getting old,
In for the kill,
Enjoying the thrill,
Turning shit to gold.

Davey's on a bar chair,
Acting like he don't care,
Ten foot tall,
Like a Wonderwall,
Not looking back in anger.

Watching the red lights flash,
When two guitars clash,
Shout and scream,
With coffee and cream,
Everybody do the monster mash.

## My Dog Day Afternoon

What happens when you get bored of life?
Bored of living the nightmare?
Alone with a friend in a glass isn't a way to live.
I don't know what to do,
Apart from enjoying every second that my feet
touch the ground.
That, for me, is the only way to be.
I certainly don't have any answers,
I can only do what I do,
Which is still breathing and being me.
That's good enough for me.
Anyone for a drink?

# Sparks and Beacons

When the sun refuses to shine,
And the grass refuses to grow,
A spark may still come,
And the land may begin to glow.

With a look that brings hope,
And a mind that brings joy,
What can you bring,
To this lonely little boy?

Will the time be easy?
Will we have to fight?
How do we know,
If we will be right?

Look to the future,
Don't wallow in the past,
Any pain that we feel,
It's never going to last.

Never trap yourself in a box,
Don't waste your time with fear,
Live the dreams and enjoy the life,
Every day of every year.

A SPARK
MAY
STILL COME...

# An Open Letter to The Past II

If I ever said that I had never loved before,
Or had never been happy with someone,
It would be a lie.
No one ever spends so long with a person if they
aren't happy.
There were times I was upset,
And there were times I was happy,
And maybe I never showed it.
There were brilliant times,
Photographs and memories of something that was,
But could never be.
Times change,
And so do we.
Everything that happened led us to be
Who we are right now.
Every scar is a souvenir,
Every line and wrinkle a small reminder of a past
time,
When we were someone else.
Memories always live on, good or bad,
And I will always think back to those days,
When I was me,
Just a different person,
You were you,
And we were us.
The same same but different.
It all goes by so fast, everything gone in the blink of
an eye,
But it is still there,

Lurking in the past like a creature in the bushes,
And I do not regret a single thing.
It made me who I am,
For better or for worse.

So, to finish off,

Thank you.

# Darmstadt

Every time I see a Lilly, I'll think of you,
All the things that you put me through,
You taught me the world and how to live,
What to take and what to give,
Even if I stood small.

You brought me happiness and tears,
Endless shots and beers,
Made me from a boy to the man I am now,
Taught me the world and how
To deal with it all.

You will always be with me,
In every thought I see,
The biggest part of my life,
Apart from kissing a knife,
But I hope I stood tall,

And did you proud.

I hope I have put a smile on the face
On every person I have met.
It's the only thing I want.
I'm not interested in money,
Or wealth,
I just want to make a difference.
If I make a person smile,
Or laugh,
Or cry,

It's the same.
It means I have made an impact.
That's all I wanted to do to you,
My second home.

## Tomorrow, Today

People cry about nothing at all,
Sometimes we don't stand after we fall,
These fears will never subside,
When everybody builds a wall.

Yesterday's tomorrow,
Is just another day,
And all these people,
Will find a way.

Got a head that's full of fears,
But these eyes won't cry tears.
The losses that we feel,
They go quiet through the years.

When you stand there on your own,
Like a child without a home.
Thinking about your life,
And what you've reaped and what you've sowed.

Take the world in our arms,
Protect everyone from harm,
When everyone wants the same,
There's no cause for alarm.

Don't think about tomorrow,
Take pleasure in today,
The people and stories,
They won't go away.

# Everything

The alcohol flowing through my veins,
The smoke that fills my lungs,
The pollutant of my world.

The happy ending I will never have,
The fairy-tale that will never come true,
The glassful of hopeless aspirations.

The smile that's spreads across my face,
The sweet sound of music to my ears,
The life in every breath I take.

Thank you.

THE DAY
AFTER THE
PLOT
BEFORE

# The Day After the Plot Before

## 1

**"T**here they are! Open fire!" shouted a voice at the entrance to the narrow alleyway.

Ken and Rachel O' Connor and William Shakespeare, facing the bright portal, turned and looked, and saw two soldiers pointing their guns at them.

To the soldiers the three figures were purely silhouettes as they were framed in the bright light behind them, but they at least knew where to aim, and aim they did.

Before Ken knew what was happening, he saw a small flash and a puff of smoke from each of the muskets aimed at them.

Shakespeare knew exactly what was going on as soon as he saw the soldiers raise their weapons, and he jumped instinctively in front of Ken and Rachel.

Ken, surprised at what was happening, stumbled backwards grabbing his wife with one hand and the Bard with the other.

Light flashed around them, and suddenly everything changed.

The dank smell of the river outside the alleyway disappeared. The silence of the small passage was replaced by groups of people excitedly chattering and shouting instructions.

Ken and Rachel knew where they were; Shakespeare dared not open his eyes.

The soldiers shielded their eyes from a flash of light, and when they looked in the alley again, they saw nothing. Darkness shrouded the area, and there was no sign of the fugitives they had been chasing and just fired at. The entire passage was deserted, and the two men looked at each other with a look of confusion on their faces, although they didn't dare to speak.

The rickety Earl of Salisbury, Robert Cecil, finally arrived at the alleyway, out of breath and limping. He had expected the soldiers to be holding the mysterious strangers that had escaped from an undercroft below the Palace of Westminster. What he wasn't expecting was to see two of his men looking confused with their muskets raised and aiming at a brick wall.

"What has happened here?" asked the Earl, struggling to get air into his lungs. "Where are the prisoners?"

His two soldiers looked nervously at each other, unsure whether to tell their master what they had seen. None of the men wanted to be the bearer of bad news and, more importantly, none of them wanted to seem insane by telling the Earl what they had seen.

"Come now! I demand an answer!" Salisbury said as he struggled to raise his voice through his shallow breathing.

"My Lord," started one of the soldiers, summoning all the courage he could muster. "The people… th-th-they disappeared! He stuttered. "One minute they were here, in the alley, and the next, they had gone. There is no sign of them!"

The Earl of Salisbury didn't know what to say as he looked down the dark alleyway and then back at his soldiers.

"Alas, people do not simply disappear! Where have they gone? I demand to know!"

"Master, they truly vanished," said the other soldier. "There was some kind of light, a flash, and then they were gone."

Salisbury looked once again into the alleyway, back to the two men in front of him then turned around, his black gown trailing behind him like a flowing shadow.

Behind him was another group of soldiers who had been following the action as they chased the fugitives from Parliament, and the Earl approached them with a snarl on his face and indicated to the other two soldiers at the head of the alleyway.

"Arrest them immediately! They are plotting against the King and I want them out of my sight!"

The two, innocent soldiers began to protest but were immediately wrestled to the ground by the larger group, and Salisbury walked off into the night, anger on his face and annoyance in his soul. He headed in the direction of Parliament, to see if he could find someone to take out his frustrations on.

# 2

Limping towards the Palace of Westminster, the anger was building up inside Robert Cecil. He was tired, annoyed, frustrated, and now he had a group of people that had apparently disappeared without a trace. It had been a long night and he didn't want to have to deal with anymore drama.

He wasn't sure what he needed to report back to the King James, although he felt that His Majesty was probably too far detached from reality to understand anyway.

He cast his thoughts towards his father, William Cecil, the Lord Burghley, who had died seven years earlier. He had been a trusted advisor to Elizabeth I, and in turn Robert had automatically become the leading minister following his father's death. When Queen Elizabeth passed away, Salisbury had promoted King James of Scotland as her successor, uniting the crowns of England and Scotland, and gaining the utmost trust of the King along the way.

Thinking back to his father, Salisbury wished that he was relaxing on his estate in Lincolnshire and enjoying a fire in his stately home rather than traipsing around the dark streets of London on the morning of November the Fifth.

As he walked towards Parliament and the entrance to the undercroft where a shower of sparks and wood had covered him moments earlier, the Earl spotted two faces that he hadn't seen in a long time, and immediately the anger inside him doubled up, and when the faces saw him, he knew the night had taken a turn for the worst.

"Ah Salisbury, have you heard the foul news of this night?" asked Thomas Knyvet, a sly smile on his face.

To his right stood Edmund Doubleday, his moustached face gazed smugly at the Earl and then at a man shackled next to Knyvet.

"And what may that be, Knyvet?" the Earl asked, not wanting to give any hint that he knew what had occurred.

"It seems as if this gentleman here was planning on a little, shall we say, incident this evening," Knyvet continued, gesturing to Guy Fawkes, who now stood outside the shattered door, manacled and guarded by Salisbury's own soldiers. "The King asked myself and Doubleday here to investigate this area, and it seems that I came not a moment too soon."

"This wretched deviant made an attempt upon my life, although I fought back and ensured that he was subdued and helpless," said Doubleday proudly, although his voice seemed to be ignored by everyone around him.

Knyvet and the Earl had never seen eye to eye as they both jostled for the appreciation and gratitude of King James, and Knyvet saw the arrest of some kind of plotter as a massive coup that would work very much in his favour.

"Indeed, I have heard the news Knyvet, for I have just been in pursuit of other characters in this scheme," said Salisbury with a suspicious look on his face, as the smile dropped from the face of his rival.

"Other characters?" asked Knyvet.

"Indeed," replied Salisbury. "It seems, my dear fellow, that the man that you have manacled here was not working alone. Fortunately, my men and I were able to give chase and corner the criminals, although they avoided capture by sacrificing themselves to the water of the river."

Doubleday stood next to Knyvet, his eyes flicking backwards and forwards between the man he had been sent out with and the Earl of Salisbury. He dared not speak as he felt the battle of egos between the two men jostling for the favour of the King.

The Earl had too much running through his head to even think about the possible truth that the people he had seen running away had simply disappeared and would much rather gain an advantage on Knyvet anyway.

"I shall leave this prisoner in your guard, and I shall continue with my duty of informing the

King of tonight's occurrences," said the Earl, as the smile that was on Knyvet's face was replaced by a look of annoyance and the realisation that he wasn't the first person on the scene of the crime.

Knyvet can have this one, the Earl thought. He had something more pressing to deal with.

How could the fugitives vanish?

## 3

"**S**o, you see Your Highness, it seems that these people, whoever they were, they just, well, they just vanished into thin air!" Salisbury found himself explaining, although he wasn't entirely sure what the King would say.

"My little beagle, that is an absolutely fantastic story! Maybe there is a book to be had out of it," said King James, oblivious to the honesty of the Richard Cecil.

"But my Lord, 'tis no story! We searched an undercroft beneath the Palace of Westminster, and found a foul conspiracy, with these mysterious people at the heart of it. And, from all accounts it seems, Your Majesty, that William Shakespeare was also involved."

At the name of the Sweet Swan of Avon the King took notice.

"Shakespeare? Why, what on earth would he be doing underneath Parliament. Oh, my dear Salisbury, what poppycock you speak! Alas, it be true inventiveness that I sense when you speak, and for all the good work that you do, if only you were honest with your findings instead of fabricating such wild, jolly japes!"

"I assure you Sir; I speak the truth. And that is not all."

He held out an object that the King looked at with a look of awe on his face. He had never seen anything like it.

Cecil had not wanted to inform the King straight away of the events of that night and had instead took it upon himself to play detective. He had immediately made inquiries about the strange people, and found out where they had stayed, while at the same time had kept upon the latest developments with Guy Fawkes.

After his arrest on that fateful night, the man calling himself John Johnson had refused to give up his conspirators, although straight away he had told the Lieutenant of the Tower of London, Sir William Waad, that he had been in contact with a group of people, a family he assumed, headed by a man they called Ken.

Salisbury used this information he had been given and, just a few hours after the drama of the early hours, searched the Duck and Drake tavern where he found strange items. Clothes made of such strange and exotic cloth, odd, small scraps of green paper with a pyramid and various pictures on it and, most bizarrely of all, a book made of paper of the highest quality, containing the works of Shakespeare.

Cecil had flipped through the book in wonder, amazed at the paper and how it felt in his hand. What was more amazing to him though was what the book contained; works that he had never heard of, from dates supposedly in the future. He had pocketed it and made his leave.

"I assure you Sir; I speak the truth. And that is not all."

Salisbury held out an object that the King looked at with a look of awe on his face. He had never seen anything like it; a book with a glossy colour, that the King couldn't take his eyes off. On it was a picture that somewhat resembled William Shakespeare, and the King ran his hands over the smooth cover.

"What is this?" he asked puzzlingly, a confused look on his face.

The King was an author himself, but he had never seen something of such high quality.

"It was found in the lodgings of our vanished prisoners my Lord. I have said that Shakespeare was with them; this is my evidence. And not only that, it has such works that we have not known about. If we ever needed proof that the fool Shakespeare was involved in some plot against you your Majesty, then I believe that this book is indeed that proof."

"I am lost for words my friend," said King James, sitting down on a chair in front of a roaring log fire, his shoulders slumped over. "How could our poet, our man of such sweet words... how could he betray me so?"

"I am certainly not qualified to answer such questions my Lord. I shall leave you in peace for this evening, and I shall return in the morrow where I may have more news for you. I hope Your Majesty can sleep peacefully in the knowledge that I will not rest until I have solved this strange mystery."

The Earl of Salisbury took his leave and left the King in peace. He got into his carriage, the strange book tucked under his arm, and headed out into the cold November night.

He studied the face on the cover intently as it stared back at him, wondering what mysteries the book held, and what it all meant.

He would head out tomorrow, or later today he now realised, as time got away from him, and examine the alleyway where the strange people had vanished, but before then he was hoping to get some sleep.

The fifth of November had been eventful enough for the short man, and his crippled body was feeling the effects of such drama. He just hoped that there was no more to come.

His hopes were soon to be quashed.

# 4

$F$rost was in the air as Robert Cecil walked along the banks of the Thames, and he could see his breath on the air as he walked the short distance from his horse-drawn carriage to the alleyway, flanked by the two soldiers who had chased the mysterious people from the Palace of Westminster the previous night. The soldiers carried torches to break through some of the mist that was starting to fall on London Town, although the candles struggled to break through the grey shroud.

His plan from the night before to get some sleep hadn't worked, as he had a hundred thoughts running through his head, ranging from the mysterious clothes that he had found, through to the even more mysterious apparent disappearance of William Shakespeare, and the discovery of a strange manuscript by the Bard himself.

He carried the book under his arm once more, feeling as if it held some connection to the mystery he was exploring. As he walked towards the alleyway where he had been huffing and puffing the night before, he found his heart beating faster, and his breathing getting quicker. His stomach felt as if it were turning cartwheels, and the nerves were starting to overwhelm him as he got closer and closer. What would he find in the alleyway?

If this group of mysterious people, however many there were, had actually vanished, there must be some trace of something, surely? But how could they just vanish? People don't do that. His thoughts turned to the room at the Duck and Drake and wondered what and who these people were.

The Earl hadn't seen them properly himself. As he had approached the undercroft the door had blown up, and the noise had been deafening. So much so in fact that his hearing had taken a while to recover, after the explosion that covered him in fragments of wood had stunned him. Cecil had seen a group of figures stream past him, but he couldn't process what he was seeing. It had all been a daze.

"It was here my Lord," came a voice from the Earl's left hand side, dragging him away from the thoughts that occupied his brain. "This is where they vanished."

Cecil stopped in his tracks and looked down the dark passageway. He could see nothing out of the ordinary although the mist was getting heavier, and visibility was bad. On the wall at the entrance to the alley hung an extinguished wooden torch and the Earl took one of the burning staffs from the soldiers to light it and illuminate the alleyway, although it remained relatively dark.

Salisbury took the torch from the wall and walked further into the alley. His soldiers gave each other a nervous look, remembering what they had seen the night before.

The Earl could see no evidence of anything untoward happening, and everything seemed as he imagined it should. Sitting on the floor to his right-hand side Cecil saw a vagabond with his head to his chest. He gave him a prod with his toe to make sure he wasn't dead, and, although he certainly didn't want to have to associate with such filth, he wondered if he may be able to shed some light on the mystery.

"You there, tell me. Did you see anything strange in this here place yesternight?"

The tramp raised his sunken head and looked at Cecil with a look of dread on his face and terror in his eye; the eye that wasn't covered by an eyepatch that was.

"A wind did blow, and a light did glow," said the hobo, looking at the Earl with a mixed expression of wonder and terror. "The earth did shake, and the people did go!"

The words sent a shiver down the spine of the Earl of Salisbury. Should he trust this vagabond? Who knows how sound and able his mind was? But then again, he mentioned some kind of glowing light, and the soldiers had talked about the same thing.

He looked over his shoulder to faintly see the silhouettes of the two men standing at the entrance of the alley, mist surrounding them and the faint glow from the torches.

"Why it seems as it should be here. I see no evidence of foul play!" said the Earl to the soldiers.

As he turned his head back to look at the tramp, he felt a low rumble. The vagabond looked at him as well, a look on his face saying that he knew what was coming, and before the Earl could ask him anything, the tramp was running down toward the entrance to the alleyway as fast as his skinny, malnourished body could take him. Cecil watched him go and noticed that his soldiers had also run away.

He looked around but could see no cause of the rumbling, when suddenly a strong wind hit him and knocked his weak body to the floor. Out of nowhere came a bright light that had the Earl shielding his eyes and then, as sudden and immediate as it had appeared, there was darkness and silence once more.

Cecil reached for the torch that lay burning on the floor, knocked out of his hand as he was felled by some unknown source. His eyes were adjusting to the darkness, but he could see the faint glow, although as he put his hand out to grab it, it raised in the air.

The Earl tried to focus his vision, and as they adjusted to the light, he could make out the outline of a pair of legs. He tried to pull himself up from the floor, and as he got to his knees, he felt a hand underneath his armpit pulling him up.

The Earl stood up as straight as his body would allow him and looked up to the person who had helped him up.

He couldn't believe his eyes. It was a face he recognized, although the last time he had seen it was on the cover of a book.

"My Lord Salisbury? Prithee tell me, can it be you?"

The Earl reached out to touch the face in front of him, checking that it wasn't a ghost. He felt that warmth of human flesh and the prickle of a short beard. His eyes rolled in his head and Robert Cecil collapsed to the floor.

Looking down at him was William Shakespeare.

He bent down as the torch lit up the small body on the floor, and beside it, a book of the Bard's works. He picked the book up, and left Cecil laying in the alley.

The words of Professor Schreiber rang in the Bard's ears; if you see anyone when you return, just ignore them. Pretend like nothing has happened. Most people will be ignorant to the unusual things in life.

As he stepped forward through the mist, Shakespeare made sure to keep to these rules. The Bard moved towards the exit of the alleyway, leaving the Earl of Salisbury behind him, and he stepped out into the fog of the year 1605.

Shakespeare was back where he belonged, and for Robert Cecil, after that morning, he would certainly remember, remember the Fifth of November.

# On Top of The World...

## And Ready to Jump

# Act 1: Johnny's Life

## Johnny Loses His Happiness

Knocked down and dragged out is how I live this
life.
If music is the food of love then my guitar is out of
tune,
And introspect is out of fashion.
I hoped that new days would bring a new me,
But today is just yesterday's tomorrow and nothing
ever changes
I wish I was the walrus,
Because Holden Caulfield is far too real.

## I See You

I saw you in the street,
And I just wish that there was something I could say
to explain
The feelings.
My heart beats for you so strongly
That it hurts me to feel this way.
Even though I try to deny it,
I know that my feelings for you are too strong to
resist,
And so I hope that the world is blind.

# Last Chance Saloon

The clock is ticking.
Must hurry.
Running out of time.
Want to be happy,
Can't miss the start anew,
Won't understand.
Fuck, almost too late.
Damn, there we go.
I missed it.

What's left for me to do now?
Everything has been and gone.
Peace and love have faded away,
And all that is left are transparent memories,
With scattered photos and words.

Someone please come and help me.
Wait, someone is coming. Maybe they can help.
Nope, he ignored me. I see a light on over
There. What is that place?
It's a pub, I think. It is! It's a pub!
Maybe they can help.
"Excuse me. Can you help me?"
"What do I want? I don't know.
Can you serve me up some empathy,
And my future in my hands?"
"No? Can you at least serve me something?
Anything?

"What's this? I can have it? Thanks very much!
Bye!"
Well, it's back to the drawing board,
Looks like the last chance saloon is shut,
But at least they were friendly.

# J.D. And Coke (Mortal Thoughts)

A thunderstorm crashing in my head,
The time has passed like lightning.
Looking back upon it all
It all seems so frightening.

The night is a blur of what could be
If I were someone other than me.
Like dead leaves fall from a tree,
Dead seconds fall from my mortality.

But we only get one chance,
Only get one life.
So carpe diem
Or love with a knife.

So I turn to the bottle looking for fun
And as I turn a light comes on.
Before my eyes it begins to sway
Please keep taking me away.

Then one day I might see,
We control our own destiny.
No sitting around hoping it will be,
Stop drinking the six-pack of apathy.

## The Face at The Window

Watching, looking, waiting.
Waiting for something to help me understand,
For someone with an answer.
Gazing out, looking for a familiar face yet
There's no one I know.
I'm just a face at the window,
Looking at numbers in the crowd.
We are all so different but in the end
We are all so alike.

## Observations of A Flame

I am simple.
A flick of the wrist,
A mere touch of a button.
I bring light,
I make warmth,
But I bring death,
And destruction.
I am simple.

## Act 2: Johnny's Anger

### The Self-Deprecation Society

The War on Terror would be career suicide
For the muppet and his lapdog in 'charge',
So a war on error is called for.
There are enough sheep in the herd
To pull the wool over everybody's eyes,
But I don't want to know what you are saying.
Telling people how to live lives
When you can't even control yourself.
Down in the street, things are out of control,
But you can't tell me what to do.
I'm an idiot for myself and no one else.

## Alien Nation

Living in a world of lies, it's hard to understand
What is happening, why it is happening.
Heads are full of confusion, soaking up propaganda.
Tension surrounds us; it can be cut with a knife.
And that's what people are doing, slicing
Their bodies and their lives.
It is hard to accept what is happening,
But even harder to do anything about it
So we cannot do a fucking thing.
With liars and criminals in charge
Everything will never be ok
And the true terrorists are still at large.

## Shadows

Death all around me,
Like millions of shadows disappearing into the light.
Yet here I am,
An undying shadow in a world of lights,
Wondering when my light will come on.

## No Good Reason

Wars are being fought
For no good reason.

The innocent die
For no good reason.

Two men planning out the future of our planet,
Just because they want power.
The twin brothers fell on that fateful day
And then the world changed.
Now as wars rage the Antichrist is coming,
Coming to wipe out humanity
So he can rule.
The Antichrist is coming
Or is he already here?

### Run

Run for your life,
Back to the East,
Where the robot is king,
And no beast
With emotion can poison the land.
Let's hurry, be quick,
No time to lose,
We have to obey,
With nothing to choose,
And every decision taken from our hand.

The monsters that dwell,
In your once perfect life,
In the brave new world,
Where feeling is a knife,
That cuts through the honour to obey.
Always around, in everything,
Destroying the once perfect you,
Nothing is how it was,
It all feels completely new,
Terrifying, this brand-new way.

# Act 3: The Happiness

## Mind's Eye

It's amazing, the visions you see
With your eyes closed.
Anything you could possibly want
And as real as you can make it.
You stare into darkness and see
The sunniest smile looking back at you.
Eyes that dance in the light can
Speak to you through blackness.
The mind's eye looking at the things you love
Is a blessing in disguise.

### Sun vs. Rain

How I love the sunny days
When nothing can keep you down
And no one can ever tell you that you're wrong.
No rain can ever touch me
When I'm covered by the parasol of friendship.

# Act 4: Short-Lived

## Intensive Cares

### I

My mind is going in so many different directions
All at once, and I don't know what to think.
A clue from you might help so I know how to feel.
Confusion is a powerful tool, blinding reality
With a jumble of thoughts.

### II

With my mind racing
And my heart beating
And my eyes aching
And my thoughts eating
Me up inside,
I'm addicted to love's sweet pain.

### III

Love, however, is only an excuse to hurt
And get hurt, and while some people are into that,
I'm looking for a lover not a sadist.
Heaven knows what I can do to help myself
When subtlety is the big difference between a
Partner and a stalker.
Maybe I'm not right for you at all.
I don't know whether to be

An Oak, a Troy or a Boldwood
To keep you interested.
I do know that I'm lost in confusion,
Like Prufrock, trapped where I don't belong.

## IV

If only I could leave, get away,
From this spell that is cast over me,
Then I wouldn't feel so lost,
Afraid at what happiness might cost.
Self-destruction is so easy,
Just be selfish, drunken, vulgar and lazy.
Either that or hurt yourself
And spend another day in perfect hell.

## V

All these feelings to not understand.
You've spoilt me for choice,
And I don't even get to decide.
That's up to you and your mood,
But please just choose so I can live and
Not worry what damage my actions may cause.

## Broken Hearts and Fresh New Starts

I'm sorry I was full of empty promises.
I never wanted it to end like this,
But somewhere along the way
We lost touch,
It used to mean so much,
And however hard we try,
We will never get it back.

When this cruel April is over,
Will the sun shine again?
Let summer surprise us,
Take away the tiredness,
Till the gleams return,
And our eyes speak with joy.

## Go Away

Bastards talk to me.

'Friends' talk to me.

I don't want to listen.

I want to be alone.

# King and Queen

The rock and roll gypsy,
She wants to dance with me,
No need for other people,
I'm the King, you see.

We go up and down, round and round,
Loving the beat of that jukebox sound,
But look closely at that Queen,
And you end up in the lost and found.

Playing that game, you know the one,
Centre of attention, desperate for fun,
Says everything you want,
But it's always a con.

Anger burns so bright in the eye,
For no good reason, don't even ask why.
Don't question a thing, nothing at all,
Accept how it is, don't even try.

A good man is bad,
The happy turn sad,
Rights turn to wrongs,
And the Queen is mad.

Little things that are done,
That once were so fun,
No longer spark in the night,
Darkness after the sun.

Time will tell, it always does,
If we were worth all the fuss.
Perhaps, perhaps not, no one can know,
If there was ever truly an us.

# Bitterness

I tried to buy a heart
I knew I couldn't afford,
And when I got rejected
It was the end of the world.
But looking back on it
I'm glad, because you're there,
Alone and I'm not.
Now just look what you could have had.
I know I'm above you now,
And you will always have to live
With the fact that I gave myself up
And would give you all I had to give,
Only for you to throw it back,
Say you don't want it when you do.
You can just live your life alone,
Because you won't have me.
Fuck you.

## Act 5: Visions

## Dreaming of Reality and The Reality of Dreaming

La Dolce Vita is what I have,
With everything I could wish for.
Love. Happiness. Money. Career.
Yet I'm pushing an elephant up the stairs,
While telling my story to an Eskimo dog-catcher.
Recounting and accounting,
Then re-counting again, faces and stones,
Bodies and sticks.
A fat man laughing.
A skinny man crying.
Envelopes looking, staring through the grass.
Torches burn like eyes in the night sky,
While I am potting and weeding away
By candlelight, kissing rain under electrical skies,
Planting photos on obscurity.
I'm aimlessly glaring at brick walls
And punching windows made of stone,
While a platypus looks on through
The windows of a stately home.
Then she cries. I feel bad.
'Take a break. Have a ball.'
But the sponge is an army of three
And just laughs while the drawer growls
'Wake up'.
So I do.
La Dolce Vita is what I want.

## Canvas of Flesh

Scars.
A permanent memory of times,
Of life, of good, of bad.
Body art of a different kind.
Knife not needle,
Blood not ink.
The effect is still the same
However, and all that is left
Are reminders of people and places,
Memories of days gone past.
Postcards of life,
Like train tickets that cannot be
Thrown away, and a journey
That will never be forgotten.

## I Just Spoke to Elvis

I just spoke to Elvis, and he is fine.
Except for one fact.
Being dead is a major hindrance
To being the King of Rock 'n' Roll.
Still, always good to know that
He's doing ok.
Oh yeah, and before I forget,
He sends his best wishes to anyone with a dog
called Stanley.
I don't know what that means,
I think he's gone a bit crazy.
Anyway, at least he can't say that
I didn't pass the message on.

# Confessions

I know there is something wrong with me,
Yet I cannot begin to describe what.
I don't know what I feel,
I don't know what I can do,
What I can say to help me cope.
Things pass me by but I don't know how.
All I try to do is get on with life,
But with everything happening around me
I don't know how I'm supposed to understand.
Do I talk?
Do I hurt?
Do I do nothing?
Only I know the answer but I also know
That whatever I do is going to be wrong.
So how do I win?
Answer: I can't.
It doesn't matter what I do because I know
That everything I do is questioned,
Is criticised, and I have to answer
To people that don't understand.
Only I know how I feel, but I don't really know.
It's not just my mind that is confused,
It is my whole life.
I want to cry out, but I want to bleed.
Do I do both and cry myself to death?
It's an abrupt end.

# Theatre

The world is a stage
And I am the show.
I'm ready to take auditions for anyone
Who wants a part.
Rehearsals on Mondays and Thursdays
While performing every day
Of the week, of the year.
No West End musicals, just ordinary theatre
With free admission but no refreshments.
Can turn into a pantomime at times.
What will the reviewers and critics say?
Who knows.
But I am the show.

(N.B. No intermission or toilet breaks)

## Act 6: Realisation

## How It Is

That wasteland right there,
Do you see?
Always standing there in front of us,
Yet we are always too blind to notice it.
It saps our life away, feeding on our needs,
And the fears we may have.
It's a harsh wasteland, but only if we let it.
Stand up, stay strong, a stiff upper lip and other
clichés,
And that wasteland we see may just become that
Eden once sought.
An eternal temptation will always be there,
But that shouldn't matter to us.
A human nature and a determination will always
lead us back.
Trees of green can cover that wasteland,
If we believe it enough.
Seventy-two something other can be there,
To join in the celebration of a blank space covered
with joy,
An emptiness filled with flowers in bloom.
One man's trash, another man's waste,
Everyone has a garden they must grow,
Let's just decide how we do it.

# You for A Victim

Just when you think that you have won,
Everything you have ever hated comes back to get
you.
The demons may be gone out of the system,
But as long as they are in the mind,
You are still not safe.

And when it comes down to it,
What more is left to write
To help you with these conflicts?
Everything sounds the same, with tales of
Sadness and Woe.

Nothing can be said anymore, to battle these
feelings.
I'm immune to all the help,
And try as people might,
Some demons can never be cured.

If things are meant to be
Then nothing can be done to change that.
The fates hold for us our lives,
And if we are destined to live alone,
To live in sadness,
To live like this,
Then there is nothing that can be done.
Try as we might to change,
If the demons of destiny have decided upon
You for a victim,

Count yourself unlucky,
For it can never be escaped.

# Hindsight

Regret fills my past
And there are so many things
That I would change.
Take it all back, stuff it in a can,
put it on a shelf
and starts a new life from fresh.

Hindsight is a terrible thing.
It makes you see where your life
has gone wrong and fucked up.

And how do we really know
when things are going to change?
Tomorrow I could be dead,
Or tomorrow I could be in love.
Life changes quickly and it's
Only after they change
That you know there was a turning point,
And you missed it.
Gone.
Left without a trace.
And you will never get it back.

## The Train

I once went on a train.
It was a cold and uncomfortable
Train but still better than some.
I thought I was the only one travelling,
I couldn't see anything else. I didn't
Even know where I was going.
It was only when I got there
That I realised everyone takes
A train to the same place.
They just go a different way.

## Act Six, Scene Five

Like a fire that burns in the hottest of winters,
An ice that will never disappear,
Chaos and creation define what will be,
Stay the night with the calmest of fears.

Fight fire with water, at an altar we stand,
A perfect moment that will never last.
A swirling catastrophe of ever-turning circles,
A reminder of the near perfect Past.

So, stay the night, together we roam.
Till the sun do us part so it's said.
Stay until morning, no need to see Rome,
The things that were once told, now lay dead.

Limitless, undying something,
No one will know what is here.
The mortal someone, the one so close,
So far and yet so near.

A weeping willow, a talk in the night,
Words that are better unsaid.
A brilliant disguise for the ones you know,
The scared, the lonely and in your head.

Stay the night, till love do us part,
The old fool that stays around.
Searching and wandering, the question that remains,
Wondering what exists underground.

Everything is eternal and stays with you
If you want to believe it enough.
Those thoughts in the mind that always stay around,
In the end they treat you so tough.

An offering to someone, a gift to a thing,
The altar doesn't care, it's happy just to see,
A care, a belief, something carved in stone.
Traitorous waves of the sea.

Perceiving the deceiving nature of it all,
A belief stands tall and tough
That beacon in the night that will never be moved,
Blown out when time has enough.

Stay the night, chill and stress out,
Castles of sand in the light.
Blow away cobwebs, laugh at the stars,
The spiders from Venus give such a fright.

Games to a joker,
Game for a laugh,
If you can never win the whole game,
At least win a half.

I see the fortune teller,
My gypsy of the night,
Feeding me words I want to hear,
But never serving right.

Our coldest of summers,
The lonely hours of sun,
Always warming the nerves
Of such a prodigal son.

Rally up those demons,
Defining who we are,
The devil in the detail
Is the one who doesn't care.

Stay the night,
Laugh forever and a day,
Until the jokes run out,
Because they don't like our way.

Dance to the silence
And sing to the sin,
Drink to forever,
But never for the win,

That will never occur.
A losing team on the side-lines,
Crying for the game,
Drowning the sorrow with buckets of wine.

A headache on ice,
Like a knife to the brain,
Let us numb who we are,
Go dance in the rain.

Kiss an electric sky,
With our minds wearing thin,
Enjoy the silence,
Such a powerful din.

So stay the night with me
One final time, before the disaster unfolds.
Always predicted, never coming true,
The story always runs cold.

# Colin's Boat Is Painted Green

It was dark as the rain fell, and a distant bell tolled three times as the sound rolled across the tree-tops and fields towards an old, grey building. Thunder rumbled through the air as lightning bolts striking down from the heavens seemed to scratch the top of the clock tower of the school building that stood out amongst the dying grass that surrounded it.

The sky was that kind of colour, that kind of grey, that you can't really describe, but you know it when you see it, that sort of thing.

The school itself seemed to come straight out of Edgar Allan Poe's imagination, gothic and daunting, dark and intimidating. It brought to mind a stereotypical mental asylum, the kind American serial killers are locked up in in films before they are inexplicably released or inevitably escape.

Inside the old building, row upon row of old school tables were occupied by elderly men in blazers and ties, caps obscuring the receding hairline and bald patches. They all stared at the front of the room like robots, unblinking and unmoving.

Amongst the elderly population of the room, standing out with his young face and short, scrawny structure, seven-year-old Colin sat at the front of the class.

Fire red hair shone like a beacon amongst the dull surroundings, as he scribbled on a blank sheet of paper on front of him. His two front teeth were missing, and he wore a dark purple anorak, decorated with small, orange flamingos.

On the desk, next to the sheet, on a cracked, grey plate, sat some mincemeat in the shape of a hedgehog.

It's a normal thing to take to school and have on a desk he had told his mother.

At the front of the class, scratching and squeaking away on a battered blackboard with a barely existent piece of worn out chalk, a teacher dressed all head to toe in black stood with his back to the non-responsive group.

He was tall and thin, with small, round glasses balancing precariously on a thin, pointy nose, A large cape flowed behind him, and a mortar board, slightly too big for his round head, kept tipping down over his face and the scratching of the chalk was intermittently interrupted as he pushed it back over his eyes.

The only sound between the squeaking of the chalk was the clacking of knitting needles as a thin, old lady sat in rocking chair next to the blackboard in the corner of the room. Her hands moved at breakneck speed as she knitted a long, black shadow, or so it seemed. Whatever it was she was knitting, it only had one colour.

The sound of her needles, and indeed her presence, was oblivious to everyone in the room apart from Colin who shot agitated looks at the lady.

Mother won't you please be quiet," he shouted, frustratingly.

The room was quiet for a second as the old lady looked up as the red-headed boy and paused for the briefest of brief moments before carrying on with her incessant clacking.

Colin rolled his eyes. The rest of the room sat and stared, not noticing or caring the exchange.

"People think I'm weird because you come to school with me Mother! Be quiet!"

The lady in the corner took no notice as she sat and carried on knitting

"Sir," Colin continued as the teacher at the front turned around. "Sir, can I have pudding now?"

"No," growled the teacher in a harsh, Scottish accent as he stared at the hedgehog. "You can't have pudding if you don't eat your meat!"

As soon as the teacher had spoken the knitting woman stood up and walked to Colin's desk. She picked up the mincemeat and threw it out the window.

Colin was surprised.

He didn't remember the window being open.

He looked smugly at the teacher as he turned and walked back to the blackboard.

"I knew there was I reason I bring you here mother. Be careful though; the baby is due any day now," Colin said as the woman walked back to her rocking chair.

Sitting down, she ignored him, picked up her knitting needles, prodded her pregnant stomach with them, and carried on with her long, monotone piece of wool.

The next day Colin was at home, playing with toy cars as an open fire burned wildly in front of him. The room was dull and bare, and shadows danced on the blank walls as the flames cast their light on Colin. The old lady sat in the corner of the room in her rocking chair once again, knitting needles in hand. The carpet beneath her chair worn away by her constant rocking.

"Do we know what it will be yet Mother?" asked Colin, but the woman ignored him. "I hope it will be a boy. Girls smell."

Once more Colin's words fell upon deaf ears and there was silence in the room, apart from the crackling of the fire and the clacking of the knitting needles.

All of a sudden there was a loud bang from the grimy window next to the fireplace. It was loud enough to make Colin jump, and he crawled along the floor to a cat flap that he had made in the wall below the window. He scuttled through the small opening and on the floor outside he saw a dirty, grey plate that was shattered, and mincemeat was scattered everywhere.

"Oh, my hedgehog," Colin said with tears welling in his eyes, until he blinked, and the tears vanished. "I will still eat it though."

On his hands and knees on the grass, Colin started picking up remnants of raw mincemeat and shoveling it in his mouth. After three mouthfuls, the food was gone, and Colin crawled back inside through the hole in the wall.

"Mother," he started, "I have finished my meat. Can I have pudding now?"

The old lady put down her knitting and stood up from the rocking chair. She walked through a large set of double doors, disguised as a bookcase, and returned almost immediately with a plate of raw sprouts that she threw on the floor in front of Colin.

He began gobbling them up off the floor, imagining he was a hungry, hungry hippo like in that game. He could never remember what the game was called though.

"Yummy pudding," he said as he hungrily ate the sprouts.

He crawled around the floor, making sure he ate every single one. When he approached the old lady who was still standing, he was shocked as a baby fell from between her legs and lay crying on the floor. He jumped towards the umbilical cord, biting it with his teeth before looking at the baby on the ground.

"It's a boy! I have a son!" Colin said excitedly as the lady sat down in her chair and began knitting once again. "I'm going to call him Anthea!"

With this he carried on gathering up sprouts until there were none left. Then he started to eat the warm rug that lay in front of the fire.

He couldn't eat it cold.


Five years later, Colin was playing with his cars once again. He had the hood of his anorak pulled up tight over his head and around his ears. On top of the hood he was wearing a mortar board that was far too big for his head, and from one corner something dripped down onto Colin's shoulder. It looked suspiciously like blood, and he took a finger, scooped some liquid up and licked it up.

Yep, he thought. Definitely blood.

The room was still as bare as it had been, except for one decoration that adorned a dark corner on one side of the room. A stuffed head emerged from the wall, and Colin looked up at it, happy that the glasses were staying on the nose.

This time there was no fire burning in the dark room and it looked slightly duller because of it;

the crackling and warmth had been replaced with a water fountain.

Colin preferred that in the winter.

Anthea was crawling around, trying to grab any toys that he could get his hands on. He was big for his age, the same size as Colin was, and his hair was just as red. The only problem was that Colin didn't like to share his toys, and he started hitting Anthea around the face with a slice of cucumber.

"Anthea leave my cars alone! I'll bite you again."

His threats worked, and Anthea crawled away from the toys.

"Can I have some mincemeat Daddy?" the boy said as he backed away.

"Of course, son," Colin replied. "You know where it is."

Anthea hopped over to the cat flap in the wall, and crawled outside, where there was mincemeat on the grass, and the remnants of a grey plate scattered around.

"Anthea is very annoying, Mother. And boring. I don't like him. I think I shall get rid of him. Like I got rid of you," Colin said as he looked at the rocking chair in the corner.

It wasn't rocking, and the knitting needles had been silenced. One end of the long black scarf was touching the floor, hanging from a lifeless hand.  Blood covered the lady's face, and Colin had placed a decorative rose in her left ear.

"So, the thing is, people bore me after a while. They are just so annoying, and boring, and annoying, and repetitive, and boring, and, oh my, you're boring me know. Goodnight."

And, after all that, it turns out Colin's boat was actually painted blue.

What are the chances?

*The Life and Times...*

## Maybe

Maybe,

You don't interest me or live in my muddled thoughts.

Maybe,

You're just a word to say when you don't have enough energy to say no.

Maybe has nothing to say to me.

Maybe doesn't exist.

Yes or no.

Now we're talking.

# Letters

My Dear Could Be,

Won't you please get back to me quickly,
With your reply to my offer.
I would so wish for you to join me at the frivolities.
I guarantee that it will certainly be such a fantastic
jape.
And if it isn't then I just don't know what I would
do.
My heart is just set on such a magnificent time with
you.
I do so wish that you will join us.

Yours,
Hopefully.

## How I Learned to Stop Worrying and Love Punctuation. Part I

Hopefully,

This letter reaches you. I wish to hear all correspondence from you. Please don't leave me alone and stop writing to me,

Never.

Could Be.

## How I Learned to Stop Worrying and Love Punctuation. Part II

Hopefully,

This letter reaches you. I wish to hear no correspondence from you. Please don't! Leave me alone and stop writing to me!

Never,

Could Be.

# An Open Letter to The Past III

For a name that shall not be mentioned,
And myself, who should be free...

I still think of you,
Of course, I do.
The only time I realised a lifetime,
Could and should be something,
And not just a shot in the dark.
A reason to believe in
Something.
Someone.
A belief passed is still a belief.
But a believer isn't always happy.

Everyone dreams
And I'm certainly no different.
Your face appears with advice
And guides me through.

Every belief is you,
As I try to be a better me

Like a star you still shine,
When the light has disappeared.

You can still make me smile.
When I think of past adventures.
And that's going some.

Do you remember sneaking outside,
Like forbidden teenagers?

Life was good.

That's the problem with dreams...

## Life and What It Entails

There must always be a Could Be,
Or a Maybe,
Or any other words disguising themselves as
Hope.
Otherwise nothing ever happens.
The future isn't written,
And life has no promise,
But it has a guarantee.
Things happen for a reason.
Let's make our story a good one hey?
Otherwise we might as well just forget about
Right now.

Happiness has missed this cynical heart once again,
And that long lost You
Is still a shadow that haunts dreams,
But it must change sometime,
It needs to.
Why not now?
It might.
Cynical me says no and I admit that.
And I am certain I am right,
For better or worse.

Doubt runs through me like alcohol on a cold
Sunday morning,
Waving goodbye to the slightest of thoughts,
A thankful goodbye kiss,
Never to happen again.

Uncertainty streaming through a jabberwocky
world,
Never making sense.
How could it?
Life is always going to be a party.
The least it could do is make some sense.

Open letters don't help,
And bright new days have become best friends
With the cauldron nights that went before.
As Mr Traubert is six sheets to the wind,
And raises his bitter head once again
The heart of Saturday night becomes a ghost
While the spirits remain bitter nobodies,
Reminding of the inevitable future disappointment
of Underdog betting.
Dancing to the silence is deafening,
And the sin is out of tune,
And out of time.

Ah time.
That coy and cruel mistress that demands and
requires us,
So easily, without giving anything back.

It's a lie if I say I had almost forgotten how much
you had plied me with false promises and a security
that would never happen.

It happens.

It's a truth when I admit it's going to happen again.
Words taken at face value and over analysed.
World enough, and time.

It happens.

Life.

Love.

It happened.

Those times,
When a cynical heart meets its iceberg.
A disaster waiting, walking.
It could change.
Could but won't.

But that Could Be must always be there.
Without it we are lost.
A tribe of Never Were's stalk the undergrowth,
Looking for that Could Be King,
Who needs to be crowned for the acceptance of life.
You will never see them,
But they need to be there.

For when that crown is surrendered
Anarchy will reign in the hearts of the thinkers and
believers,
And the purge will begin;
Non-believers and under achievers will reign terror
over what might have been,
And Could Be is resigned to backwards thoughts
And lines etched on life.

Hopefully sits with a mind elsewhere,
On thoughts to come and events to pass.
Something to never happen
But that must surely be why he's called Mr H?

But then again, never mind the Never Were's,
What about the Never Could Be's
And their ghosts that forever linger
Behind our eyes.
A tiny shadow clouding
Mr Could Be
As we look upon him,
And all of those possibilities that
Will never come true.

# ON A COLD SUNDAY MORNING...

# Flowers

In a world in ruins,
In a city of dirt,
There are flowers in the crack of the street.

In the beginning of tomorrow,
At the start of what was,
The crossroads where two lovers meet.

The petals that grow,
When the rain comes down,
Through the gap in the clouds of defeat.

The bright new tomorrow
In a world going wrong,
Sitting in the victory seat.

For when it's said and done,
And after habits are blown,
They stand on shoulders, not feet.

Two lovers as one,
Star-crossed but never afraid,
Flowers in the crack of the street.

## Ghosts

I'm a ghost that haunts the corridor I used to walk,
Only seen by few,
And nothing like it was.
Cast over by the gazes of strangers
Who take the place of everyone you know.
Times change and so do we,
But forget who we used to be.
Talking and walking,
Regretting and forgetting.
Ponder what Could Be,
Never thinking about Maybe,
Just pawns of our cruel mistress.
Sapping away at memories of old,
When it's easier to leave it alone.
Days turn to things that you can't remember,
And never miss,
But you can't get back,
And we look to the future with rose tinted glasses.
Glasses full of numbness as each day becomes a
future past that slips away without notice.

## Love is Freedom

Punk doesn't care who you are,
What you do,
Who you are,
Who you do,
What you are.
We are the same,
Regardless how an orange cloud covers us.
And anti-social media may tell us,
We are people.
We are the same.
Years ago, a working-class hero
Told us,
We are all together...
We have no reason to let the world tear us apart
When all we care about,
Is Us.
It's a truth with
Everyday proof.

LOVE
IS
FREEDOM

## S.W.

A smile that melts an icy heart,
And eyes that show such compassion.
Picking me up when I'm down,
Keeping me safe from harm,
And making the world right.
Letting me feel like a child again.
Thank you for being you,
And making me
Me.

# Going Underground

## 1

Scooters zoomed past Ed Taylor as he walked down the dark, grimy streets of the old town of Naples, and all of his senses were being overwhelmed.

The smells of the fresh pizza and pastries from nearly every shop he walked past; the sounds of the incessant beeping Vespas and the multitude of chattering in so many different languages; the bright colours outside every shop, but mostly the red of the *cornicelli*, the chili pepper-shaped lucky charms that adorned every shop, stall and street seller; and the taste of the ice cream he was eating.

It was the best in town Ed had been told. It just tasted like ice cream to him.

Ed had been in Naples for four days, the second time he had been there since a school trip some 16 years earlier. He had loved Pompeii, and the story of Vesuvius erupting, and returning to the area was something he had always wanted to do.

While Ed had walked around the many excavations and museums in the previous days, he thought he would see what Naples had to offer, after enjoying the friendly but overpriced neighborhood of Sorrento.

His first impression of Naples and his walk from the train station wasn't the best. Ed was thinking about biscuits mostly, thanks to the eternal name of Garibaldi that confronted him wherever he looked, and when he had finished searching on his phone for the best way to walk, he was amazed at the amount of rubbish on the streets. Everywhere he looked, sofas, chairs, shoes and suitcases were piled up on street corners and on the side of the roads.

He was admiring the complete lack of courtesy and sanitation when his thoughts were interrupted by a car pulling up on the street next to him, and instantly depositing a cardboard box and several drinks can on the floor next to him, before promptly speeding off.

Charmed, I'm sure, Ed thought, looking up from the small glow of his phone, before staring intently once again at the map. He wanted to memorize it as much as he could, so he didn't have to keep looking at his phone. It didn't seem to be the best area to keep a new top-of-the-range smartphone in the palm of his hand.

Confident he knew where he was going, he pocketed his digital map, pulled his jacket collar up and tried not to make eye contact with anyone.

The weather was colder than he was expecting in mid-April, although it had been predicted there would be thunderstorms when he was there and he had only experienced one, and that was on his visit to Pompeii.

He had enjoyed being in the forum of the ancient ruins, looking up at the mountain that had caused so much destruction while the sky rumbled ominously.

Although dry now, there was still a chill in the early evening air as Ed strode as quick as he could though the crowds of tourists and natives that seemed to line the street in equal measure.

His brown square glasses fell down his nose as he hurried, causing a blur over the top of them. Ed hated his eyesight, his virtually blindness through shortsightedness and his dependence on glasses instead of contact lenses, but the eye infection he had recently recovered from meant that he was stuck with his geeky specs for the time being.

Ed stopped on the way, taking the time to check the map to make sure he was going the right way. The streets all looked similar and the souvenir shops all looked the same. He realized he was almost where he wanted to be, and his attention was snapped away from his phone by a scooter beeping at him. Ed moved quickly to the side of the narrow street as the Vespa sped past him, and almost into a car pulling out of one of the even narrower side streets.

Making sure he was safe from kamikaze moped drivers, Ed walked through a small piazza with a large church on one side and the mandatory pizza restaurants and souvenir stands on the other. He looked around a corner and saw what he was looking for: *Napoli Sotterranea*. The underground tour of Naples.

He had read about the tour online and in the small hostel he was staying in it had been recommended to him. A guided tour through a small network of tunnels leading to various bunkers and underground reservoirs was right up Ed's street. He just thought it was a shame it was guided. He would love to explore underground to his heart's content and see what he could find.

Ed had been on various journeys and trips to abandoned places, from the Communist Party Headquarters in Bulgaria, to an abandoned Mr. Blobby theme park in Somerset, and spent countless hours on urban explorer websites, looking for places to explore and investigate.

He had been told about various nooks and crannies that it was possible to go down in the caverns under Naples, even if you weren't meant to, and that's when he had an idea. Carl, the stoner Australian that ran Six Small Rooms, the hostel where Ed was staying, had told him that some of the guides don't count the guests, and just expect them to be OK.

It was a wonder no-one had gotten lost down there, Carl had said. Ed didn't plan to get lost, but he was going to explore.

The queue in front of him was huge, but he bypassed the crowd with the arrogance that the English seem to possess abroad and strode up to the young man that was addressing the group.

"I'm here for the English tour," Ed said.

"Sorry, the last English tour is fully booked," said the long-haired man with a twang to his Italian accent. "Tomorrow, you come back."

Well this has put the balls in my plan, Ed thought to himself.

"Come on mate," he started. "it's only me on my own. I'm leaving tomorrow."

It was a lie, of course, but he didn't know that Ed figured, and lo and behold, it actually worked!

"OK," the guy said hesitantly. "go quick."

He ushered Ed through where he quickly paid his ten euros and walked down a set of stairs to a large stone room awash with English speaking voices. There wasn't as many people as Ed was expecting, although there were still around 25 people by his reckoning. As everyone waited around, English being spoken with various accents, Ed stayed away from the group as much as he could. If no one really noticed him to start with he would have less trouble slipping away, that was his plan.

Ed looked around the room and noticed the uniformity of the clothes that surrounded him. He looked down at the tan and maroon checked trousers that he was wearing, the ones that friends and family lovingly named the Rupert the Bear trousers and wished he had worn something a little more inconspicuous. Hopefully he wouldn't stand out too much he thought.

Time would tell.

## 2

$A$s Ed sat on the stone bench that went around the edge of the room, he was a world away, lost in his own thoughts, when he was interrupted by the tour guide introducing himself. It was the same man that had let him through. Ed hoped he wouldn't pay much attention.

"Good evening ladies and gentlemen, my name is Toni, I'll be your guide tonight. I'll just give you a little idea of what we are going to do, what the tour is, and then we start, OK?"

The words that flowed from Toni's mouth flew straight past Ed's ears without stopping as he tried to avoid eye contact with the tour guide.

As the group got up to move, Ed made sure he was towards the back, where it would be easier to slip away.

They started off in an old quarry, where Toni the tour guide gave them a brief history of the cavern they stood in. Ed had to admit to himself that the history behind it all was interesting, certainly more so than he had expected, and when he stood in a large room with dusty children's toys that were left from World War II, Ed certainly started to feel slightly emotional. His stomach was fluttering, though, at the thought of what was to come.

As the tour progressed and passages between caverns got tighter, Ed felt his heart beating faster and faster as he got closer to where he wanted to be. He had asked Carl about the details of the tour, about the gaps and the passages, wanting to know as much as he could.

He could have just gone on the tour first to find out for himself, but then again, he wasn't made of money. That was his reasoning anyway. The ten euros entrance fee could be used much more productively he thought to himself.

As the group came to an area Ed had heard so much about, the candlelit tour, he braced himself. Toni gave a brief history of the room and after a short intermission they carried on. It wasn't candlelit anymore of course; that was far too dangerous for the modern health and safety standards. They now used small torches designed as candles, although that had been a very late modification.

The idea of a group of thirty strangers walking through passages barely narrow enough for small children, carrying naked flames, well that idea all seemed well and good for the Italian authorities, until they realized that it was very much one of the worst ideas since a strange movie director had decided to put nipples on the Batsuit, and they swiftly put an end to the candle tradition.

There was an emergency exit this time, as the groups moved forward, with the tunnels being so narrow. Ed wanted to make sure he got to the back of the group, so he didn't get seen by any hesitant wanderers, and by the time they had picked up the faux candles and walked past the exit, his plan had worked. He was the final person in the group, and he kept his distance from the giggling posse in front of him.

They were close enough that he could see their dark silhouettes and hear their soft, German accents, but far enough that they weren't paying attention to him, and why should they?

He was just another shadow in that dark, stony corridor.

As he looked up and down at the small alcoves in the walls where Toni had explained that workers back in the day had scuttled along like spiders, he came to an opening on his right-hand side.

The entrance to the gaps in the rock seemed wide enough for Ed; he wasn't the biggest of men after all. A simple red and white tape was the only obstacle in the way. Top of the range security he thought.

Ed briefly doubted himself and thought about whether he did actually want to explore the underground tunnels, break countless laws and God knows what else. These thoughts lasted for a very brief second until instinct and excitement took over.

He looked at the cackling group of German girls in front of him, not paying attention, and, after a brief glance over his shoulder and making sure he wasn't being observed, Ed stepped over the plastic rope and into the small chasm in the rocks.

## 3

$T$he first thing Ed felt was excitement. Nerves didn't exist. He was alone in a narrow tunnel that seemed to be getting smaller as he walked.

Ed felt like Willy Wonka as he walked towards the chocolate room. He didn't need to play Rachmaninoff on a miniature piano though. He didn't need to play any tune as a matter of fact. He just needed to duck until he was hunched over like some kind of Parisian legend with his fake candle barely illuminating the darkness in front of him. It had been quite light in the previous tunnels, although they had electric lights in them.

Now Ed was in the sole company of the darkness the light seemed a lot dimmer. Taking his phone from his pocket to turn the torch on, he stopped as he struggled to get the screen to react. The occasional slowness of technology annoyed him, although he always swore by it when he had company.

The torch on his phone flicked on although it didn't make a big difference to the suffocating darkness, and after a few seconds, Ed's tapping at the screen caught up as the bright light that shone through the dark tunnel suddenly disappeared.

As Ed attempted to illuminate the tunnel once again a light flashed behind him and he saw a silhouette on the wall in front of him, like a creepy shadow puppet.

He turned around as quick as he could in the cold, narrow corridor, fumbling with his phone as he did so. Turning around as the beam came on, the phone slipped out of his hands and fell to the floor. The torch lit up the space in front of him, where Ed half expected to see Toni the tour guide giving him a lecture in his broken English, but to Ed's surprise there was no one there.

He held his breath as he tried to hear any footsteps that may be nearby but the only sound that came to Ed's ears was the noise of his deep breaths, and the slight scratch of small stones underfoot.

Bending down to pick up his phone Ed blew the dust and small stones from the back of it, and then looked at the front, only to see a crack on the top left corner next to the front camera. Typical he thought, although on the flip side it wouldn't be a modern phone without being cracked like everyone else's. That was the in-style nowadays it seemed.

As he pocketed his now-trendy phone, Ed turned around as he tried to get his bearings and carried on his journey. He wasn't so far into the maze of tunnels that ran under the city, but the adrenaline was starting to run, and his heart was beating fast as he started to wonder where the flash of light had come from. His thoughts were soon interrupted as he came to a small opening in the smooth rocks on his right. The tunnel carried on in front of him, but he stood at the junction wondering which way he should go.

Despite his curiosity telling him to go through the opening, Ed resisted the urge and carried along the larger tunnel that he had been following. He hadn't walked for long when his phone torch stopped reflecting off the narrow walls that surrounded him and instead became duller as the tunnel expanded into a large cavern.

This one was darker than the ones on the tour, as the lights that had been installed to help tourists see were absent. Ed pointed his torch to the floor as he walked along the path the went around the side of the room. The stone turned into a small bridge that ran over a now-empty stream, opening out into a large, bare, stone lake. The water had long since gone now the caverns were now longer used as reservoirs, although Ed was certain he could hear the flowing and gushing of water nearby. Probably from one of the rooms on the tour Ed thought. If he could hear that, then they wouldn't be far away, and he would have to be extra careful he said to himself.

Ed stopped halfway across the bridge to shine the torch around the immense space around him, although there was nothing to see as the light was smothered by the darkness that surrounded him. His eyes were adjusting to the lack of light but in such an immense area Ed couldn't make out a single shape, although there wasn't much for him to see apart from the walls of rock.

Ed shone the torch in front of him once more, lighting up the path he had yet to walk, when he heard a noise from ahead of him. It was only a small tap, but it was sounded louder as it echoed through the emptiness that surrounded Ed. He flashed the torch around and something on the floor caught his eye. A small flash of light reflected back at him.

He walked towards it, light glinting off the object as he approached with his torch. Ed wasn't sure what it was, but it was small, black and rectangular. As he got closer, he realized what was reflecting his torch, and then he knew that the path he was treading had been recently walked. As he stood over the black object, standing out in the pale rubble that made up the floor, he bent down and, placing the white, artificial candle he was still carrying on the floor, picked it up.

In his hands he held a smartphone, remarkably similar to his own. He turned it over to look at the screen, although there was no power it seemed, as he touched a button on the side of the case, and nothing happened. The make was the same as Ed's though. Exactly the same in fact. Same brand, same type.

And then Ed noticed the crack.

He flipped his phone around and held the two objects side by side and looked at the lines that ran down the screen from the camera.

It was an exact match.

## 4

$E$d had been looking forward to his adventure under Naples. He had visions of exploring and discovering long-lost treasure and could see himself emulating Indiana Jones.

What he hadn't foreseen was the fact that it was going to be difficult to navigate the long and winding, narrow tunnels. He hadn't thought about how he was getting out again but reckoned he could make it from the cavern he found himself in. Apart from the tunnel he hadn't gone into, there was no other way to go.

Ed wasn't going to take any chances anymore though and picked up a small stone from the floor and, using it as makeshift chalk, drew an arrow on the wall next to him, pointing behind him before putting the stone in his pocket.

As Ed looked down at the two phones in his hands, he wondered where the other one had come from. The crack on the screen was in the same position as on his phone. But then again, a crack is a crack, and many phones had similar patterns on them. He looked at the floor behind him and noticed his footprints on the ground. He followed them with his eyes as he shone the torch. His prints followed him to where he stood, and were the only steps visible on the ground, but to his surprise, when he looked in front of him,

Ed noticed a single pair of footprints entering the tunnel ahead.

He double checked behind him, but sure enough, only his footprints were there. Checking his arrow on the wall and pocketing his candle, Ed shone his torch ahead of him and carried on his journey.

The next tunnel took Ed up a steep slope, and he found himself slipping slightly as he walked up it. Not being in the tour, there were no safety rails to hold on to, and the rock faces next to him had very few grooves to grip on to. He struggled up the slope, but eventually managed to reach the top. Ed's phone flashed as the torch decided to turn itself off for no reason, and Ed cursed loudly as he stood at the top of the narrow tunnel. He unlocked the phone, his cold fingers swiping an E-shaped pattern on the lock screen, then turned the torch on again.

Ed gasped as the torch lit up a face in front of him, and as he gave out a yell in surprise and amazement, his hands flew in the air, and the phone flew backwards out his hands. He looked behind him as the light fell through the air before landing on the slippery slope where the light got dimmer and dimmer as it slid down, until Ed heard a small tap as it landed on the gravel.

He reached into his pocket and took out the fake candle, flicking the on switch on the bottom as he did. The faint glow in front him lit up a strange painting on the wall of a misshapen face with pointy teeth showing from an open mouth.

Ed ran his fingers over the painting, wondering about the history behind it. It was for discoveries like this that he had been looking forward, and he wished he had his phone to take a picture of it.

Holding the candle closer to examine the picture, Ed noticed some writing underneath the gruesome face; *tempus edax rerum*.

It was Latin Ed guessed, although he had no idea what it meant, and he decided to go and get his phone so he could get a picture. He just hoped that it hadn't been damaged as it fell.

He turned on his heels and marched down the narrow slope, trying his utmost not to slip and slide his way down, although it would be quicker, he thought. The way down seemed longer than the way up, but through the dim light of the torch Ed could see the bottom of the tunnel.

As he put his foot down, Ed entered a large cavern once again, and he began to look for his phone. It couldn't have gone too far from the where he stood, he reckoned.

His thoughts were disturbed by a tap at the end of the chamber. He walked towards the sound, and saw a small black object laying on the floor. He looked behind him, but the way he had come was too dark to see anything.

Confused, Ed walked towards the object and picked it up.

It was his phone. The same make. The same crack. He pressed the button on the side, but nothing happened.

Ed looked around him, confused. He thought he might be getting cabin fever, hallucinating, but it all looked real enough. As his eyes scanned the darkness for traces of anything that he might recognise, he suddenly became fixated on the wall next to him.

There was a small arrow drawn with a stone. It pointed at the way that Ed had just came.

He looked behind again, and saw two sets of footprints, while ahead of him, in the dim light he could make out a second set leading forward.

He followed them.

# 5

$\mathbf{A}$s he walked up the narrow, slippery passage once again, Ed's mind was racing. He must be imagining it he thought. Perhaps he was claustrophobic, and his mind was playing tricks on him. He tried to put these thoughts out of his mind as he walked up the greasy route, although he still had a nagging feeling at the back of his mind.

His thoughts were still racing when he realised that he had been walking for longer than he had done previously, when he came face to face with the painting that had shocked him, although as soon as the thought entered his head, the tunnel levelled off. There was no sign of the painting though. Ed looked around him, in case he had missed it, but nothing was in sight through the dim light that the candle torch was sending out.

He took the small stone out of his pocket, and scrawled another rough arrow on the wall, pointing in the direction he had already walked, then stumbled a few steps further on the level floor. Silence surrounded him except for the crunching of stones underfoot.

As he walked forwards, Ed felt the floor taking a downward slope, and he followed it until he entered a large room yet again. A massive sense of déjà vu came over him, although everything looked the same in the darkness anyway. Even so, Ed had a bad feeling as he walked the path that lay in front of him.

He looked to his left-hand side and a sense of inevitability came over him as his eyes scanned the wall until they found what he was expecting and dreaded. He looked from the arrow and down at the floor, already knowing what was going to be there.

This time was different though. Next to the battered phone on the floor lay something else. Ed couldn't quite make it out in the dim light, but as he got closer a feeling of dread came over him.

Ed recognized the Rupert the Bear, checked pattern on the dusty cloth, and his heart skipped a beat. He was sure he was hallucinating and was intent that he wasn't going to succumb to the repetitiveness of the cave.

He looked down at the old reservoir next to him, now empty except for the darkness that was beginning to get thicker with each passing moment. It didn't seem so far down in the dull light, although it was hard for Ed to tell. He reckoned it was about the same distance down as one he had seen earlier and decided to risk it.

What's the worst that could happen he thought to himself.

Jumping over the side he fell a few metres and his left ankle rolled and cracked as he landed on the uneven, rocky surface below him. A sharp twang of pain ran through Ed's leg and he gave out a short yell that bounced off the stones around him and echoed in the empty chamber.

He turned the dim torch in the direction of the bridge he had jumped from and headed in that direction. The water had once flowed in this way, so Ed guessed there would be a passage out, and fumbled in the darkness as he walked towards what he hoped would be an exit.

Ed tripped over a couple of times as the light of the artificial candle seemed to get swallowed by the gloominess around him. He limped and stumbled as he walked over various sized stones and rocks, until the light illuminated a small tunnel, and Ed struggled to climb up the small mound that covered the entrance.

His ankle was giving him massive discomfort, and as he reached the tunnel Ed took the opportunity to sit and have a rest. He tried rotating his foot, but the pain was too immense.

He stayed there for what was probably only a few minutes but to Ed seemed like a lifetime. He had lost all concept of time and regret had started running through his mind.

Struggling to stand up, he shone the torch ahead of him as he hopped up a small incline. It was then that the torch started flashing as the batteries decided that they had had enough and didn't want to work any longer.

As they gave up the ghost and left Ed in total darkness, he carried on up the small, narrow tunnel, feeling his way on the walls with one hand while holding the other out in front of him.

Ed's heart pounded as his fingertips stretched out in front, still holding the torch that he had relied on, felt the coldness of the stone wall that was in front of him, and as Ed brought the other hand out in front of him, it confirmed his worst fears. His first thought was that maybe it was a wall he could climb over, or there might be a way through somehow. He needed to see first though.

Shaking at the lamp, Ed stood next to the wall, hoping and praying that it might have a little bit of power left but to no avail. He decided to try the old rubbing the battery trick and flicked the cover off the battery case on the underside of the candle. He took the cell out, gave it a rub on his dirty t-shirt, and put it back on before replacing the cover. He flicked the small switch, and to Ed's astonishment there was light!

Any hope that he had, though, was quickly vanquished by the site before him, and the pointy teeth and dark eyes stared at Ed as the light from the torch disappeared once more, and before he knew it, Ed's consciousness fell into darkness as his strength slipped away from him and he fell to the floor and down the slope behind him.

He rolled to the bottom, his limp ankle flailing behind him as he went, until he fell with a crunch upon the small stones. Ed managed to open his eyes briefly as he lay on the ground and picked his head up off the floor to look around, but it was all a blur. His glasses had fallen off his nose, and Ed had no idea where they were.

The torch had decided to light itself once again, and as Ed tried to shake off the groggy feeling in his brain, he looked at the floor next to him, squinted and manage to make out his small broken phone sitting there once more.
Ed managed to turn his head and look down at his ankle, hoping that the searing pain would disappear, but as he saw the outlines of the unnatural position his foot was in, he lost hope.

His Rupert the Bear trousers were the last thing he looked at as he closed his eyes, and the vision of the face entered his mind. He thought of the Latin writing, not knowing what it meant, and then breathed his last breath.

$\mathbf{E}$d had been looking forward to his adventure under Naples, and as he broke off from the small group in front of him and down a side branch, excitement ran through him….lights flashed, and a silhouette appeared…the trousers his family had lovingly name Rupert the Bear trousers…the torch flickered as the batteries gave up the ghost…his glasses fell over his nose…he saw a face looking back at him from the wall…Ed had been looking forward to his adventure…Rupert the Bear trousers…a light flashed…he looked at the crack of his phone…a silhouette appeared…a face looked back at him…Ed had been looking forward…the torch flickered…he heard a thud in front of him…he saw some writing…a silhouette appeared.

Ed thought of the Latin writing as he closed his eyes. A sense of déjà-vu came over him. He wished he knew what it all meant and drew his last breath.

*Tempus edax rerum;* Time, devourer of all things.

## THE END

# Author Notes

So, in November 2019 I went on a Punk Rock cruise in the Caribbean, organized by a band called Flogging Molly.

It was fantastic, and special, and absolutely beautiful.

It was a weird and random thing to do I guess but there you there, and on this cruise I met some wonderful people, and listened to some amazing artists telling fantastic stories, and I thought, well why the hell don't I just go through some of the stories, anecdotes and inspirations for where the poetry and stories in this book come from.

Some come from people, some from places, but all from experiences, because, at the end of the day, we are all living in a story and an experience, in everything we do, every day of our lives.

Anyway, I'll get straight to it and I'll try not to ramble.

Oh, and there will be some constant themes in these stories, namely women, Darmstadt in Germany, and alcohol.

Lots and lots of alcohol!

So, we start with **Dance**.

I remember going to work in an Asian restaurant in Darmstadt one morning, and as I was 5 minutes away I got a phone call saying "hold on, don't come in yet, it's a bank holiday, we don't open for another 2 hours" or something along those lines.

Now, for those who don't know, in Germany bank holidays aren't just on a Monday like in the UK, which is what I was used to, but they can have them on any day of the week, and for anything!

Seriously they will say, "it's a Thursday and we invented beer once, let's have a holiday!"

Anyway, I had lived in the country for ten years at this point, so I was used to their weird ways, but sometimes I swear there are days where they just make stuff up, but I was hungover as well, so let's put it down to both things.

As I got the call I couldn't bothered to go back home, although it wasn't far away, but went for a cup of tea, and started writing. I had written the first couple of lines a long time before and hadn't really done anything with them, but on that day, stuff just came out.

And then it came to the ending.

This was inspired by a couple of sources, one modern, one not quite so.

I'm a fan of Steven King, and I'm a huge fan of time travel, so when I found out about a book of his called 11.22.63 I knew I had to check it out.

The brief synopsis is that a man travels back in time to prevent J.F.K from being assassinated. I won't say anymore about it for fear of spoilers but then came a TV adaptation as well, and at the very end, without giving anything away, there is a speech, or rather a poem, read at the end:

*We did not ask for this room, or this music;*
*We were invited in.*
*Therefore, because the dark surrounds us,*
*Let us turn our faces toward the light.*
*Let us endure hardship to be grateful for plenty.*
*We have been given pain to be astounded by joy.*
*We have been given life to deny death.*
*We did not ask for this room, or this music.*
*But because we are here, let us dance.*

The first time I heard it I had tears running down my face and I thought, if I could ever write anything so beautiful, I could die a happy man, so, I tried...

And most likely failed, but it's the trying that counts right?

So that was a modern influence. The other one, slightly more obscure, comes a from a Russian Anarchist from the late 19th/ early 20th Century by the name of Emma Goldman.

Now for those who don't know of her I suggest looking her up. She was an incredible, fantastic, forward thinking woman who championed and advocated women's rights, gay rights, and the rights for freedom overall, essentially, but anyway, as I say, you can look her up and read more.

The story goes once, that she was at a dance and one of her peers reprimanded her for having a good time, basically, saying that it did not "behoove an agitator to dance" so afterwards Emma Goldman wrote a letter of beliefs:

'I did not believe that a Cause which stood for a beautiful ideal, for anarchism, for release and freedom from conventions and prejudice, should demand denial of life and joy.'

Years later, in 1973, a transcript of this was sent to a printing merchants in order to make some t-shirts with Goldman quotes on, and the printer took her words and turned them into the most famous quote that she never actually said but which has inspired so many people:

"If I can't dance then I don't want to be a part of your revolution.'

And there you have it.

*For you and me,*
*For the World around us,*
*For a revolution,*

*Let us dance.*

Now we come to **_Just A Shadow._**

This short story goes back to a script that I wrote at university with Philip Roberts and Steven Prior. We were coming up with ideas for a short film, and one night I had a dream about an old man dying and seeing an alternative life.

Now this was the time when Johnny Cash had just released a song called 'Hurt' and it was played everywhere. The last lines of the song are 'if I could start again, a million miles away...' and I guess hearing that fairly often imprinted in my memory because there I was, dreaming of this idea. I went to Philip and Steven the next day and presented my idea, and I was shocked when they actually thought it seemed good.

We ended up doing some rewrites and came up with a script that we filmed for a short film called Shadows in Bright Light. The title came from the fact we wanted to set it in Las Vegas, and we liked the idea of trying to get funding to take us over there. It didn't work, so we relocated the thing to London, and filmed there.

Writing the story, I guess I could have relocated it back to the original location of Vegas, but I know London better than I know Las Vegas, so I kept it as it was. As I wrote I could remember the fun we had, writing and shooting the film. I don't think there are really many stories behind the filming , but it was an important time in the development of my writing I think, and going back to write it as a story enabled me to get some little details in there, like the *'Outatime'* easter egg, which I had actually completely forgotten about until now!

**Tomorrow, Today** is a collection of two halves really. The first half is quite negative, quite downbeat, and we won't spend much time on those. The poem of the same name, we will come to that later, and go somewhere more upbeat.

As to the first half, **Hey You** and **Open Letter to the Past I,** these could be two parts of the same thing essentially. I went through a breakup in Germany, and it left me feeling quite angry and upset, which is only natural I guess, but I never had chance to say things I wanted to say, which made it worse in the end, and so these two were born of that anger and frustration.

Neither of them are things I am particularly proud of them, but they are a snapshot of where I was at that time in my life, and almost a reminder to not go back there again. After writing these I heard some words that I try to emulate and live by, and so there is an apology for these writings later on, but more on that one later.

One thing I did learn though, was not to be angry and horrible to people, no matter what they have done. It's just a waste of energy and in a world where there is so much negative energy, there's no pint in adding more. That's pretty much all there is to say about these. I won't mention any names, as anyone aware of what happened knows it and who was involved, so moving on!

Let's head to the middle of that collection, and to **Cauldron Nights... And Bright New Days.**

These were intended as two sides of the coin, where the nights relate more to the darker connotations that it has, and days obviously to the more positive.

Tom Waits. For those who have heard of him, has been a massive influence on the train of thought writing that goes into some of my work, those drunken ramblings if you will, and he is referenced here with Traubert, from his song Tom Traubert's Blues, but the whole thing was written with one eye on his work. *The Heart of Saturday Night'* is such a fantastic album, with is descriptions of late-night bars and drunken characters, and that is something I tried to emulate, or at least reference, here.

The title of Cauldron Nights comes from a bar in Darmstadt called Kessel. Now this is a bar that is open until 5am sometimes, and is one of the places to go when everything else is closed, and as such you meet all kinds of people there, and a kessel, in German, is a cauldron, or at least a large pot, but Large Pot Nights didn't have the same ring to it for me, so Cauldron Nights it was.

There isn't much more to say about that writing, I guess. It's about drinking until the early hours of the morning, the people you meet doing it, and sometimes, just sometimes, the friendships that form in those wee, small hours. Some of those I will touch on later, with other stories.

The Bright New Days, that follows Cauldron Nights, I wanted to reflect the first writing but with the positive spin on it. I tried to keep some of the ideas, the themes, and the words the same, but using a different point of view.

In the collection the two poems becoming the link between the positive and negative aspects, and as such I wanted them to act as a turning point.

Moving on to **An Sibin**.

The An Sibin was an Irish Pub in Darmstadt where I worked for ten years until the owner went bankrupt, and as such I met so many crazy, weird and wacky people out there, as well as some of the best friends that I could ever have asked for.

Some of the verses, while referencing songs, such as *Chelsea Dagger* by the Fratellis, have nothing to do with the pub except for the fact we played the songs there, but a lot of them come directly from bands related to the pub, all of them friends of mine.

The opening comes from a singer called Florian Grey, who at the time of writing this is based in Hamburg. Now a solo artist he was previously in a band called Eve's End, and wrote songs called *Serpent Eyes* and *Frozen Heart Philosophy*. Flo is a fantastic mate, and I travelled over to Hamburg once to surprise him at a concert, and it was a brilliant time. I think it's little memories like that that you can look back on and smile. It was a special night.

The line about 'you can save my soul' comes from an unfortunately now extinct band called the Beatshots. Emma, the singer, is from Portsmouth, and the guitar player and synth guy Benny was a partner in drinking crimes when I first started working in the pub. They were a fantastic band that were doing synth-indie music, and one of their songs was called *'We Will Save Your Souls'*.

'Lucy and her rock and roll' and 'living like outlaws' reference a fantastic band called The Barbers who released an album called 'Outlaw Pop' and a song called *Lucy Loves Rock and Roll*.

The Barbers actually played at my leaving party when I left Germany to move back to England in 2017, and I joined them on stage for *Lucy…* and they changed the lyrics of some of their songs to reflect me leaving, and it was that night that I realised that I was actually quite liked over in Darmstadt!

It was a moving night, and quite life affirming, in that it was one of those moments when you realise the positive impact that you can have on people, and vice versa.

Then we come to 'Davey dancing on a bar chair'…

This guy deserves an award for still being alive after some of the stuff we did together, nearly all of it involving alcohol.

First of all, he was a big Oasis fan, hence the references there, but I walked into the pub once and found him in the office listening to techno music, with a towel very loosely wrapped around his head. I didn't know what to say when I looked at him, and I think he knew what I was going to ask.

"I'm a fucking shepherd man! Got a towel on me heed!"

Well, say no more!

I turned and walked away and went behind the bar to grab some papers I needed to copy, and next thing I know I heard a huge fucking bang, and I ran through to our smoking area and there's

Dave, laying on the floor with the towel next to him, bar stool sideways at his feet.

"What the fuck happened?" I asked him.

"I was dancing and fell off the stool dickhead!"

Fair enough.

We had a lock-in once, and started listening to music at stupidly loud levels and consuming unhealthy amounts of alcohol. For some reason, we had lots of condoms behind the bar, and I'm not entirely sure why.

We used to hold a big student induction there one Monday night every October, so its possible they were left over from the goody bags left behind, I can't be sure, but what I do know is I was sitting at the bar with my favourite Bulgarian, Georgi, a man who's friendship has been immense and who I am eternally grateful to for the support he has given me, and all of a sudden Dave has walked up to us and he's trying to pull a condom over his head.

Well, I didn't really know what to say so I just watched.

It snapped.

Well, if at first you don't succeed...

I think he went through seven or eight condoms with success until he gave up, but each attempt was strangely hypnotic as this drunken, bearded, absolutely crazy guy from South Shields attempted some kind of self-asphyxiation.

We went to a football match once, watching Darmstadt play, and there was us two, singing songs about a player called Marco 'Toni' Sailer, who was a friend of ours, when we got told to be quiet!

We got told to shut up. In a crowd of 18,000 singing people. In a football stadium.

Well this didn't sit well with Dave, and from that point on the person who had told us to be quiet was met with some very English profanities from thereon in.

In our defence, everyone else was fine with our songs, and some of those around us joined in, but from that point onwards, that lone warrior who objected to our singing got a quiet shout of 'wanker' after every chant in the stadium.

It was one of those that made senses at the time. I still see Dave when I visit Darmstadt, and we still go for drinking sessions, but nothing like we used to.

I would say that we are both growing up and becoming more sensible, but I don't think that will ever properly happen.

Well, hopefully not anyway.

**Darmstadt**, a city that became a massive part of my life, is about a place that I will never forget. I moved there in 2007 to visit my sister and ended up staying for ten years. I couldn't speak a word of German when I got there, and left with the previously mentioned leaving party, dancing in the middle of I don't know how many people, a Fleur de Lis, the emblem of the city inked into my skin, and having become an English Heiner, the Heiner being a Darmstadt native.

It was an honour to become part of the history of the city, and the thing is, I did make a difference. I won't be written into the history books as someone who did something special, but I know there are people that smile when they see me, and if I can get a smile everywhere I go I will certainly be a happy man.

The friendships I forged there are still going strong, and on every return, I am welcomed back with open arms and love as if I have never been away.

If you have never been, and get the chance to, you will experience a vibrant city but the centre has a closeness and mentality of a small town in terms of community and friendship, and I highly recommend it.

The last poem from the collection I will talk about is **Tomorrow Today**.

In my time in Darmstadt and in the An Sibin, I worked with a guy from Cuba called Julio Hierrezuelo, who has an absolutely stunning singing voice. He is one of those people that is always smiling, and his happiness at life is infectious. We spoke once about me putting some words to his music, and so he sent me a couple of instrumentals and I wrote some lyrics, and he did some demoes.

I have mp3s somewhere on my computer of a few of these. I know there was one called 'All My Life', another called 'Underground', and one called 'Funk Heaven', which was about being together with a girl, realising she is boring, and then getting together with her sister because she is more open to threesomes. I think that song is available online, as Julio recorded it with people from around the world.

Anyway, instead of Julio writing music and me sending lyrics, I came up with some words and sent it to him. He made a tune and put the lyrics to it, and floating around somewhere is a demo version of that song as well, using the first 2 verses of the poem.

I ended up writing more and realised after the first part that it kind of fitted in within the little concept that I thought about, and so that tiny idea was born.

There is a singer called Will Varley, who writes some of the most beautiful lyrics in the world, in my opinion, and he wrote a song called *To Build A Wall*, and I think it was this song that was at the back of my mind when I wrote *Tomorrow*...

I saw him at a tiny venue in Wiesbaden, with chandeliers hanging from the ceiling and I think there was only about 30 people in this little place, and when he sang that song, it was heartbreaking.

Such a beautiful tune.

Will also performs a song called *Seize the Night*:

*Seize the night,*
*Do your best to lose track of time,*
*If you know where you are when you wake up,*
*Something's wrong.*

I lived by that for many years, both before and after I had heard the song.

As I said, a lot of my previous time and stories include alcohol. I always felt I was living a rock and roll lifestyle, just without the money, but always with a disregard to everything else. When he sang that, it kind of hit a nerve that having a good time involves drinking.

It took a while until I realised it's not always necessary.

It makes it more fun though.

**The Day After the Plot Before**, I wrote this as a little follow up to 'Outatime' for a couple of reasons.

It was only after writing the book that I realised I had missed the part of Thomas Knyvet out of 'Outatime', and after all of the reseatch I had done for the story, I was slightly annoyed with myself. He may not be the most well-known of people, but he had a larger part in the larger unveiling of the plot than I realised, so I wanted to try and rectify a wrong there.

Plus, I didn't want to get moaned at by history bods.

Anyway, at the end of Outatime,

SPOILERS HERE SO READ ON AT YOUR OWN RISK!

The family get transported back to the modern day in front of the soldiers chasing them in 1605, and I myself wondered what happened to the soldiers after this?. What would happen to them, and how would life go on? That's when I decided to do a mini-sequel, just to explore what happened after the O'Connor family disappeared. It was a little idea, and I think in the end I just wanted to revisit 1605 once again.

Moving on to the next collection of poetry, **On Top of the World: and Ready to Jump,** and this I intended to be a story, telling the life of 'Johnny', whoever he is. In truth, I think he was me at 16 and 17 when I started writing the poems, and then as I went through university, but at the same time I think the themes of joy and loss, love and pain, they are universal so I maybe there is a bit of us all in there somewhere.

In the collection there is a poem, rather over dramatically, called **J.D. and Coke (Mortal Thoughts)**. Now this was the first actual thing I really wrote as an adult, or as much of an adult as a 16-year-old can be, outside of school, and I remember it as if it were yesterday.

In 2001 we went on a school trip to Greece for a Classical Civilisation field trip, and it was there that I got drunk, as the title suggests, on that famous Tennessee mash, but being 16 years old, I felt the need to be melodramatic about it, and sitting on the back of a coach travelling through Greece I wrote what would be the first of many it seems.

That was really the only reason I wanted to include it. I don't like it particularly but seeing as how it is kind of how everything began then I thought I might as well leave it in.

As mentioned previously, some of these poems were written during my youth, some during my university years, and a few were written during my time in Darmstadt. **Observations of a Flame, Run** and **King and Queen** were all written during those years in Germany, and all concern the subject of the anger at the beginning of the poems.

I remember actually writing the latter two during arguments in restaurants, in the various toilet breaks where I was given a bit of peace and quiet. I can't remember what the arguments were about, probably nothing, but sometimes the writing always seems to stick with me longer than the inspirations.

**Dreaming of Reality and the Reality of Dreaming** was my attempt at writing some kind of nonsensical verse using inspirations from around me. I had various posters hanging up in my bedroom at university and most of them are referenced in there, as well as that famous REM lyric. I always liked the idea of the norm mixing in with the absurd, and this seemed to me to relate to dreams and what they can often do in terms of taking you to strange, unrelated places.

I think most of the verses in this collection are mostly quite simple and as such there isn't much to really mention about them, however being some of the first things I had written and containing various segments of my life from the age of 16 through to 32 it kind of seemed kind of fitting to put it here in this book as it is a somewhat rather large snapshot of my life.

The final poem in this one, **Act 6, Sc. 5** is mish mash of various and random thoughts, but deliberately so. Apart from the first two stanzas, which were written at the same time, each of the others were written in various states and emotions, as in I was waking up mornings and writing a single verse, and as such I think they switch between happiness and sadness, anger and joy, and obviously there are many hangover thoughts in there.

I did say that alcohol is a dominant theme running through this entire book!

This is one of the poems with the most musical references in it I think, ranging from Bruce Springsteen to Green Day, David Bowie and The Beatles. There are many more references, far too many to mention, so have fun finding them!

I didn't have another name for it, although I think 'Stay the Night' was one I toyed with for a while, but in the end I think I was just too lazy to think of anything else, so in the end I just stuck with the initial working title.

And that brings us to the end of the second collection!

The next short story, **Colin's Boat is Painted Green**... well what can I say about this one??

It's a strange one and I'm not entirely sure where the idea came from. I do remember writing a short script for it originally and sent it to a friend of mine who is an animator, in case he wanted to do something with it.

Looking back, I don't think I ever got a reply from him about it…

I wrote it as a throwaway piece when I was trying to get back into the flow of writing after a hiatus, and I guess I just wanted to make it a bit dark and a bit weird.

Fun fact: Originally Colin was named Luke, after a song by a band called Great Big Sea called *Lukey's Boat*, and Anthea was called Lucy. Years after I wrote the original idea with these names, my sister gave birth to children a couple of years a apart; a son called Luke and a daughter called Lucy.

Just one of those coincidences that life shows you it seems.

Then we come on to the latest poetry collection, and probably the last one I will write; **The Life and Times of Could Be, Maybe, and Other Stories.**

At one time or other, we all think 'what if' don't we? Or think about how life could have been? I think it is another thread that runs through this entire book, from 'Just a Shadow', to 'Hindsight' and through this collection as well.

The first poem I'll mention is the third **Open Letter to the Past**. The anger and pain I spoke about earlier seemed to overwhelm me at the time, and I let it get to me quite often. I used to dream about the girl, and it weighed quite heavily on my mind all the time.

And I then I heard a song. The sentiment was so simple, and so wonderful, but it made a difference. I started to realise that there wasn't any point in being caught up in the past, and letting the anger dictate me or boil up inside me. The world around us has so much anger and bad craziness in it, so why should we add to it? This song spoke to me, with three simple words, and they helped to change my mentality for the better; Be More Kind.

I am a big fan of a singer called Frank Turner, with lyrics from him inked in my skin, and his music has helped me through different situations in life.

A song called *'Get Better'* became an anthem for me during a break-up and still serves to inspire happiness and resolve in me, but when I first heard *'Be More Kind'* it really did change my mindset, and I decided to do and be just that.

I wrote the third 'Open Letter...' as an apology for the previous things I had said, and not long after writing it I did have the chance to see the ex-girlfriend who had influenced it, and I did show her it.

After that I had no more dreams about what had happened, and it felt like I was able to move on.

It was a great feeling.

So, 'be more kind' has almost become a mantra for me, and I think that if more people did believe it, we would be in a better place as a human race. It sounds like a very idealistic thing, I am fully aware of that, however the sentiment itself is so simplistic that it really shouldn't be so difficult should it?

**Life and What It Entails**, is the culmination of all the poetry collections in this book. I wanted to wrap up all the ideas and references together, going from 'Cauldron Nights' through to 'Act 6, Sc.5' so there are references to these in there, as well as the 'carpe diem' poem of Andrew Marvell from the mid 1600's, *'To His Coy Mistress'*.

I think it is quite a varied writing, and I don't remember much about writing it. It was written over various days and nights, most likely sitting in a pub somewhere, but apart from that there isn't much to say about it!

The next four poems are almost extras, unrelated to the ideas that went before, but each of them have a meaning behind them from the latest chapters of my life.

**Flowers** was written as for the wedding of my sister and brother-in-law. In a world that seems to be going to shit, they have four fantastic children that give me some hope that the future won't be all bad.

Remember that Asian restaurant from the beginning of all of this? After moving back to England and going to visit Darmstadt, I went there to say hello, only to realise that there was no one working there that I knew any more. All the faces had changed, and no one knew who I was, so I sat at the bar, had a drink or two, and wrote **Ghosts**. Reading back on it, I guess it is somewhat related to the others, with mentions of 'Could Be' and 'Maybe', but I wrote it after everything else and so I class it as being outside of the ideas, although they were references put in to try and link things.

I wrote **Love is Freedom** in Blackpool at a punk festival called Rebellion.

Now I believe that the punk music scene has the most incredible sense of unity and community, and the first time I attended this festival I couldn't believe the feeling in the air. There were people from all backgrounds, ages and races, some with pink mohawks, some skinheads, some grandmas, some children, but every single person was the same.

I have never felt anything quite like it, and I go each time to remind myself that, much like the 'be more kind' sentiment, it is so easy to get on with one another.

For a few days in August in that seaside town, the world is tiny and united, and it is fantastic.

I'm going to come back to that idea shortly, but first I will just talk about **S.W.**

This was inspired by the very latest chapter in my life, and I hope, as these words live in, that it is a chapter that long continues!

It was written for a girl that helps me to improve myself in everything I do, who lets me go crazy and supports my stupid ideas and who is still there at the end of the day, with a hug and an ice pack, and such loving words.

As with the others, I won't mention names, but she knows who she is, so I shall say to her, thank you.

The final short story, **Going Underground**, was inspired by our own holiday to Naples that I went on with S.W. Now I have never been with someone that really likes history and culture, and as such most of my holidays have involved beaches and sun, but for our first holiday together in April 2019, the aforementioned S and I decided to go to

Italy. I had been once on a school trip in 2003 and loved it, but she had never been. Anyway, we went to Pompeii and Herculaneum, climbed Mount Vesuvius and generally had an amazing time.

Before we left we decided to do a tour of underground Naples, and it was very much like I describe it in the book. Very small gangways, extremely dark, but opening into these huge caverns.

They used to use them as bunkers during the war, and as such there are still some personal artifacts of the people that were down there, including children's toys, which brought me to thinking about what happened to them, but children in wartime is something that I don't think I will ever be talented enough to write about, but a young man getting lost, now that I can handle.

Hopefully.

Anyway, our tour guide did actually tell us that some of the guides don't count how many people are in the group and just assumed that they were all there, and that got me thinking about someone getting lost, and built the little story from there.

Most of the details are autobiographical, from the 'Rupert the Bear' trousers to Ed being in Naples on a school trip, and the thunderstorm in Pompeii.

That really was an ominous feeling, looking at Vesuvius while the sky rumbled.

Great times.

And now, going back to punk music uniting people, and the thing that inspired me to write this little background on some of the stories in here.

I went on the punk rock cruise in November 2019, and the feeling I got on that boat was like that of Blackpool. There was a massive sense of unity and love, and it was fantastic, and during the time there I met some fantastic people, as well as having the honour to meet some of the people who have influenced me over the years. I met Jake Burns, the legendary singer of Stiff Little Fingers, after an acoustic, solo concert he gave, where he had told stories from throughout his careers, and before that Frank Turner, who had done something similar telling stories about the historical women featured on his album 'No Man's Land', and it was listening to these that I wanted to write about some of the people, places and influences behind some of the words in this book.

And with that, I will finish.

The Salty Dog Cruise of 2019 that inspired me to write this will live on in, as will the people on that boat in the Caribbean who let me be part of their lives for five days.

Thanks to all you Shipmates out there.

This one is for you.

Printed in Great Britain
by Amazon

82150351R00128